Félix Houphouët-Boigny

Ohio Short Histories of Africa

This series of Ohio Short Histories of Africa is meant for those who are looking for a brief but lively introduction to a wide range of topics in African history, politics, and biography, written by some of the leading experts in their fields.

Steve Biko
by Lindy Wilson

Spear of the Nation (Umkhonto weSizwe): South Africa's Liberation Army, 1960s–1990s
by Janet Cherry

Epidemics: The Story of South Africa's Five Most Lethal Human Diseases
by Howard Phillips

South Africa's Struggle for Human Rights
by Saul Dubow

San Rock Art
by J. D. Lewis-Williams

Ingrid Jonker: Poet Under Apartheid
by Louise Viljoen

The ANC Youth League
by Clive Glaser

Govan Mbeki
by Colin Bundy

The Idea of the ANC
by Anthony Butler

Emperor Haile Selassie
by Bereket Habte Selassie

Thomas Sankara: An African Revolutionary
by Ernest Harsch

Patrice Lumumba
by Georges Nzongola-Ntalaja

Short-Changed? South Africa Since Apartheid
by Colin Bundy

The ANC Women's League: Sex, Gender and Politics
by Shireen Hassim

The Soweto Uprising
by Noor Nieftagodien

Frantz Fanon: Toward a Revolutionary Humanism
by Christopher J. Lee

Ellen Johnson Sirleaf
by Pamela Scully

Ken Saro-Wiwa
by Roy Doron and Toyin Falola

South Sudan: A New History for a New Nation
by Douglas H. Johnson

Julius Nyerere
by Paul Bjerk

Thabo Mbeki
by Adekeye Adebajo

The Truth and Reconciliation Commission
by Mary Ingouville Burton

Robert Mugabe
by Sue Onslow and Martin Plaut

Albert Luthuli
by Robert Trent Vinson

Boko Haram
by Brandon Kendhammer and Carmen McCain

A Short History of Chinua Achebe's "Things Fall Apart"
by Terri Ochiagha

Amílcar Cabral: A Nationalist and Pan-Africanist Revolutionary
by Peter Karibe Mendy

Wangari Maathai
by Tabitha Kanogo

Josie Mpama/Palmer: Get Up and Get Moving
by Robert R. Edgar

Female Monarchs and Merchant Queens in Africa
by Nwando Achebe

Mozambique's Samora Machel: A Life Cut Short
by Allen F. Isaacman and Barbara S. Isaacman

Chris Hani
by Hugh Macmillan

Kwame Nkrumah
by Jeffrey S. Ahlman

Privileged Minorities: A History of Wealth Concentration in South Africa
by Mesrob Vartavarian

Félix Houphouët-Boigny
by Marco Wyss

Félix Houphouët-Boigny

Marco Wyss

OHIO UNIVERSITY PRESS
ATHENS

Ohio University Press, Athens, Ohio 45701
ohioswallow.com

Printed in the United States of America

Ohio University Press books are printed on acid-free paper ∞ ™

Library of Congress Cataloging-in-Publication Data

Names: Wyss, Marco author
Title: Félix Houphouët-Boigny / Marco Wyss.
Other titles: Ohio short histories of Africa
Description: Athens : Ohio University Press, 2026. | Series: Ohio short histories of Africa | Includes bibliographical references and index.
Identifiers: LCCN 2026021470 | ISBN 9780821427125 paperback | ISBN 9780821427132 pdf
Subjects: LCSH: Houphouët-Boigny, Félix, 1905–1993 | Presidents—Côte d'Ivoire | Politicians—Côte d'Ivoire | Côte d'Ivoire—Politics and government—1960–1993 | Côte d'Ivoire—Foreign relations | LCGFT: Biographies
Classification: LCC DT545.83.H68 W97 2026 | DDC 966.68051092—dc23/eng/20260422
LC record available at https://lccn.loc.gov/2026021470

For my son, Lawrence

Contents

Illustrations

Maps

Figures

Acknowledgments

I am very grateful to Tony Chafer for reading the first complete draft. His extremely helpful comments and feedback have allowed me not only to steer clear of inaccuracies but also to improve the overall readability of the book. I would also like to thank the two anonymous peer reviewers, who through their comments enabled me to further contextualize Félix Houphouët-Boigny's life and political career and strengthen the book's relevance. Any remaining mistakes or omissions are of course solely of my doing. I would also like to express my gratitude to Arthur Banga for his help in getting access to photographs, and for our continual exchanges on all matters on and related to the Ivorian leader and Côte d'Ivoire. Finally, I appreciate the generosity of the Fondation Félix Houphouët-Boigny in providing me with a selection of photographs to illustrate this book.

Abbreviations

AOF	Afrique occidentale française
IMF	International Monetary Fund
OAU	Organization of African Unity
OCAM	Organisation commune africaine et Malgache
PCF	Parti communiste français
PDCI	Parti démocratique de Côte d'Ivoire
RDA	Rassemblement démocratique africain
SAA	Syndicat agricole africain
SATMACI	Société d'assistance technique pour la modernisation agricole de la Côte d'Ivoire
SDECE	Service de documentation extérieure et de contre-espionnage
SFIO	Section française de l'Internationale ouvrière
SODERIZ	Société pour le développement de la riziculture
SYNARES	Syndicat national de la recherche et de l'enseignement supérieur
UAM	Union africaine et Malgache

Introduction

> Houphouët-Boigny is objectively the most conscious resistance to the evolution and liberation of Africa.
>
> —Frantz Fanon, summer 1960

In summer 1960, the French Martinican psychiatrist, writer, and freedom fighter Frantz Fanon (1925–61) was serving as the ambassador to Ghana for the provisional Algerian government, the government-in-exile of the National Liberation Front. In the country of Pan-Africanist Kwame Nkrumah, the future author of the anti-colonialist *The Wretched of the Earth* was in the first row when the decolonization wave swept through sub-Saharan Africa (hereafter Africa) and seventeen colonies emerged as independent countries in a single year. In this "Year of Africa," Côte d'Ivoire too gained its independence, from France, with Félix Houphouët-Boigny (1905–93) as its undisputed leader and president. Moreover, that same summer, the Ivorian leader was in a standoff with French president General Charles de Gaulle because Houphouët-Boigny wanted independence on his own terms and without strings attached. It thus begs the question why Fanon, as quoted above, felt he had to single out Houphouët-Boigny as the main stumbling block to the successful decolonization of Africa and, in sum, as an African traitor. Was Fanon influenced by his host, Kwame Nkrumah, who was not only a regional rival of Félix Houphouët-Boigny but also competing with him over their countries' economic and social development—and, more broadly, Africa's future—following a wager they made in 1957?

From a West African perspective, and certainly also from a francophone African one, the Ivorian president had not distinguished himself as an African nationalist in the years leading up to independence. On the contrary. During the 1950s, he served in successive French governments and, as a minister, helped shape, defend, and champion two major schemes to save France's empire: first the *loi-cadre* (framework law) and then the French Community, which successively and gradually gave the colonies more internal autonomy while retaining them under Paris's yoke. Moreover, and this must have been particularly offensive to a representative of the Algerian freedom struggle like Fanon, the Ivorian leader spoke out against the independence of Algeria. Even in the wake of his country's independence, he continued to uphold France's control of the North African country. The days when Houphouët-Boigny was celebrated for his anti-colonial politics thus seemed to have long gone. Indeed, as a recently elected member of the French National Assembly in 1946, he had played a key role in the abolition of forced labor in the colonies. Even at the time of Fanon's writing, the Ivorian president succeeded in forcing de Gaulle to grant Côte d'Ivoire and its allies from the Council of the Entente—Niger, Upper Volta (now Burkina Faso), and Dahomey (now Benin)—independence without the prior signing of neocolonial cooperation agreements. Also, Houphouët-Boigny had not yet become a key figure in *Françafrique*[1] and, relatedly, in France's neocolonial sphere of influence in francophone Africa—a.k.a. the *pré carré.* This would lead the Ivorian president later to be labeled as "France's man in Africa."[2]

In trying to make sense of Houphouët-Boigny, however, we cannot divide him into chronologically different characters, ranging from an idealized young freedom fighter to a diabolized old neocolonial stooge. The complexity of his character and politics transcends different periods of his life and career, defies categorizations, and calls for nuance. His previously mentioned standoff with de Gaulle during the transfer of power illustrates this particularly well. Retained as a minister in the French government when the general returned to power in 1958, he had been an architect and key advocate of the French Community, which he believed provided the ideal protected and supported space for the economic and social development of Côte d'Ivoire. But when this vision and the Community came crashing down after de Gaulle had given in to the Mali Federation's demand for independence in late 1959, he made a virtue out of necessity. Instead of accepting independence on French terms and facing humiliation after having supported France's imperial agenda, he projected himself as an African nationalist. Yet, he had not given up on developing his country under France's protective umbrella. Once he had achieved the ostentatious independence he had wanted, Abidjan and the other Entente capitals negotiated and entered into tailor-made cooperation agreements with France.

This episode and outcome, which thwarted de Gaulle's attempt to dictate the postcolonial relationship to France's former colonies, illustrate two interconnected ambiguities at the heart of Houphouët-Boigny's political life. First, while he saw himself as a key partner of France in Africa and was generally supportive of the former colonial power's African agenda and world role, he also ruthlessly pursued what he considered to be in the best interest of Africa, his country, and himself. Second, while he usually looked to Paris for guidance and assistance, he also exerted substantial influence over policymaking in the Élysée.

Houphouët-Boigny was both an independent leader and a French asset, and his relationship with Paris questions the power dynamics within *Françafrique,* which Antoine Glaser has suggested be turned on its head and instead called "AfricaFrance."[3] Although France was the theoretically stronger side in the equation, and often called the shots, the Ivorian leader had considerable power, which manifested itself not only in Abidjan's relations with Paris, but also in Ivorian, West African, and African affairs. Coupled with authority, this power was initially rooted in his lineage and social position, but he then astutely expanded, strengthened, and consolidated it through his education, professional development, economic enterprise, and politics. In so doing, he pragmatically, sometimes opportunistically, and certainly astutely, leveraged local, regional, and international situations and constellations. This allowed him to multiply his power and to have a profound and lasting impact on his country, region, and continent, as well as on Franco-African relations. In light of this legacy, and his half-century-long political career, it is thus surprising that until this book there has not been a single biography of Houphouët-Boigny in English.

The lack of a direct interest in this key figure of twentieth-century Africa in the English-speaking world can to some extent be attributed to the scholarly divide between anglophone and francophone Africa. Yet another potential reason is, to creatively paraphrase Aristide R. Zolberg, that studying the Ivorian leader and his country was not "cool." "Revolutionary" leaders and countries, such as Nkrumah and Ghana, often held more appeal for scholars.[4] This pattern seems to have transcended scholarly generations, from Zolberg's in the 1960s to today's.

Meanwhile, with a seemingly steady and enduring political career, he lacked the dramatic international exposure of figures such as Congo's Patrice Lumumba, who tragically came to embody the devastation wrought by the twin forces of neocolonialism and the Cold War. Moreover, Houphouët-Boigny did not offer the same degree of scholarly accessibility and familiarity as anglophone African leaders, and, unlike in Côte d'Ivoire and the francophone world more generally, he did not appear as directly relevant. Consequently, it was within the francophone sphere that scholars, as well as those he worked with and against, took a particularly keen interest in Houphouët-Boigny.

In addition to books on specific aspects of his life and politics, this interest has also led to some biographies. The main and most balanced one is Ivorian scholar Frédéric Grah Mel's magnum opus, completed in 2010 and consisting of three momentous volumes.[5] This thoroughly researched biography is an invaluable source on the Ivorian leader, but its sheer length, seemingly encyclopedic nature, and extensive quotations make it not particularly accessible. The other major biography on Houphouët-Boigny, meanwhile, is shorter and thus somewhat more accessible. Yet Paul-Henri Siriex's biography—both the first and the updated version were published during Houphouët-Boigny's reign—reads more like a hagiography.[6] Siriex's political and business roles in francophone Africa brought him close to the Ivorian leader, for whom he clearly developed an admiration.

Partisanship is a real problem in the French-language literature on Houphouët-Boigny more generally. While his allies, supporters, and admirers have tended to elevate him into an almost saintlike figure, detractors, political opponents, and enemies have portrayed him as a villain. What all works on or related to Houphouët-Boigny have in common, however, is that they attribute to him significant agency and influence in the destinies of his country and Africa. Where they mainly differ is on how to interpret his motivations, policies, and actions, and whether they were, ultimately, morally right and beneficial for his people and Africa. The literature also deals with one or more of the complexities that this biography aims to address. They are, in addition to the previously mentioned ambiguities in his relationship with France, his African nationalism; his vision for Côte d'Ivoire and Africa; his views on subregional and regional roles; the regime; his economic and social agendas; and his relationship with religion and architecture.

In contrast to Fanon's accusation of 1960, the perception of Houphouët-Boigny had been markedly different in the immediate postwar period—both in Africa and the metropole. Many Africans saw him at the forefront of the fight for freedom, and French politicians and colonialists feared him as a dangerous pro-communist agitator. In leading on the legislation for the abolition of forced labor in the colonies in the French National Assembly, he was politically allied to the communists. But this earlier political record, like his later one, should not be taken at face value. The Ivorian leader defies binary classifications. He was neither for communism nor against African emancipation. Houphouët-Boigny's African nationalism was very different from that of such African leaders as Nkrumah, and this was reflected in his vision for Côte d'Ivoire and Africa. Once he had allied himself to the French ruling class in the early 1950s, he wanted to develop his country as a constituent part of a reformed French empire. Instead of outright independence for the colonies in Africa, he preferred to see them—to some extent in line with late-colonial thinking in Paris and London—evolve under the umbrella of the metropole. When independence became the only option available to Houphouët-Boigny with the implosion of the French Community, he nevertheless wanted to remain, despite a temporary effort to burnish his African nationalist credentials, in a strong, cooperative, and almost exclusive relationship with France.

This lasting proximity to France led such Pan-Africanists as Nkrumah and his former political ally Ahmed Sékou Touré of Guinea to accuse him of being a neocolonial stooge. Meanwhile, Houphouët-Boigny also clashed with African nationalists and Pan-Africanists over the future of the subregion and region. Whereas they advocated West African and continental integration, he pursued subregional and regional cooperation, predominantly of an economic nature and with Côte d'Ivoire as the *primus inter pares*. This clash of visions for his country and for the continent also placed Houphouët-Boigny in what was considered, in Western Cold War parlance, the camp of pro-Western moderates, as opposed to pro-Eastern radicals, in Africa's Cold War. In both regional and East-West terms, the Ivorian leader was therefore a controversial figure who, as a result, had not only admirers and supporters, but also vociferous critics and enemies. In order to shield his country, regime, and, especially, himself from any real or imagined enemies, the Ivorian president established an authoritarian one-party regime and cracked down on any potential political opponent. He did not fit, however, into the category of the ruthless and brutal authoritarian dictator, for he did not execute any supposed conspirators and even reintegrated some of them into his regime and Ivorian society.

Houphouët-Boigny also actually seemed to care about the well-being of ordinary Ivorians and for the economic and social development of Côte d'Ivoire. But he believed that for this development he needed France's support and protection, the Western capitalist system, and a tight grip on the Ivorian population. In combination with Côte d'Ivoire's resources, this recipe seemed to work. Houphouët-Boigny oversaw what was, in the immediate decades after Ivorian independence, considered an economic miracle and thus seemed to have come out victorious from his wager with Nkrumah about the development of their respective countries. This very economic success allowed the Ivorian president to invest in social benefits and infrastructure, making Côte d'Ivoire a showcase for France's cooperation policy in Africa. Yet he also used this wealth for his own benefit and the pursuit of a religiously motivated vanity project, the gigantic Basilica of Our Lady of Peace in his hometown, Yamoussoukro. The Ivorian president was a devout but religiously tolerant Catholic. This tolerance was necessary in a country that had not only indigenous faiths but also, due to labor immigration from neighboring Upper Volta, a growing Muslim minority.

By the time the basilica was consecrated by Pope John Paul II in 1990, however, it was questionable whether the "old sage" had gotten his policies right. Following an economic crisis, the country found itself in an increasingly dire political crisis. In the wake of Houphouët-Boigny's death in 1993, this crisis—which pitched his political heirs, historical political opponents, and ethnic and religious groups against each other—escalated, and by 2002 had spiraled into a civil war. The "Ivorian crisis" officially ended in 2011 after the forceful resolution of the post-electoral crisis that followed the triumph of Houphouët-Boigny's former prime minister Alassane Ouattara over the "old sage's" long-term critic and opponent Laurent Gbagbo. But it remains questionable whether Côte d'Ivoire is out of the woods.

The rationale for this biography is thus not only to fill a major gap in the literature and to address the complexities and seeming paradoxes in Houphouët-Boigny's long political life, but also to question his legacy and long-term impact on Côte d'Ivoire. More generally, following the path of this simultaneously eminent and notorious African leader sheds light and provides insights on many key episodes of modern African history, ranging from the world wars to decolonization and the forced liberalization towards the end of the twentieth century, and on other important themes, such as postcolonial political, social, and economic development; Africa and African countries in the international system and, relatedly, African agency; and France's enduring role in Côte d'Ivoire and the region.

In order to look at the history of twentieth-century Africa through the life of Houphouët-Boigny while simultaneously trying to provide a more holistic and nuanced picture of the Ivorian leader, this short biography is divided into four chronologically and thematically driven chapters. The first one will retrace Houphouët-Boigny's early life from his birth into Baoulé nobility at the beginning of the century to his emergence as one of West Africa's foremost leaders following the Second World War. The second chapter will then analyze his conversion first into a major advocate of and player in France's imperial project in Africa, and then temporarily into a vociferous African nationalist following the implosion of the French Community and during the negotiations for the postcolonial relationship with France. The third chapter will present the Ivorian president's machinations as a "cold" warrior—mostly in partnership with France—in pursuing a regional leadership role, notably against Ghana's Nkrumah, in supporting separatist Moïse Tshombe in the Congo, in assisting Biafra during the Nigerian Civil War, and in reaching out to apartheid South Africa. Finally, the fourth chapter will focus on his domestic policies, and thereby shed light on his increasingly authoritarian excesses in collusion with France, the economic and social development of Côte d'Ivoire, his infrastructural endeavors, and his country's descent into economic, social, and political trouble in the last years and days of his life and reign.

Houphouët-Boigny's story is told on the basis of both primary and secondary research. But in light of the desire for a brief, accessible biography and the need to synthesize and nuance often polemic writings, references are provided only for quotes and when specifically referring to an author. For those interested to take their readings on the Ivorian leader further, there is a bibliography at the end of this book.

1

The Making of a Leader

> A lot has indeed been written about me, very beautiful things. If there were errors, they were not made in bad faith, but in ignorance of the facts and the very nature of our society.
>
> —Félix Houphouët-Boigny, 1988

When Félix Houphouët-Boigny looked back on his life in 1988, his twilight both politically and biologically, he clearly seemed aware that his hagiographers had tended to make exaggerated claims about him, particularly about his origins. One of these claims was that he was a descendant of the eighteenth-century queen Pokou, an Ashanti princess who founded the Baoulé Kingdom and thus its people, a subgroup of the Akan. In reality, the only established commonality between the queen and the Ivorian president was their belonging to the same ethnic group. This and other myths about him resulted not only from the imagination of his admirers and those who wanted to ingratiate themselves with him, but also from his own frequently cryptic and misleading statements about his origins and early years. This issue was further compounded by the fact that his birth and childhood had hardly, or not at all, been documented. Although he grew up during the heyday of French colonialism in Africa, the reach of the colonial administration inside Côte d'Ivoire was still limited in the early twentieth century.

It was only in 1893, after more than a century of intrusion and interfering, that France officially established Côte d'Ivoire as a colony, which in 1904 was integrated into the federal imperial construct of French West Africa (Afrique occidentale française, AOF) with Dakar in Senegal as its capital (see map 1.1). Full, formal colonial status did not, however, equal full colonial control. French attempts to expand the empire's authority from several strategic footholds were often met with violent resistance. It was only through the methodical use of force that France managed to quell the defiance to its rule and came to be largely in control of the Ivorian territory on the eve of the First World War. The future Ivorian leader was thus born into a world where the traditions of Baoulé society were still heavily present, and the French colonial apparatus was still being built, its policies only gradually affecting young Dia Houphouët—as he was originally called—and fellow Ivorians. Nevertheless, born into a family of hereditary chiefs, he was pulled into France's colonialist project and an assimilationist agenda designed only for a select few. Starting with primary school in his village, he climbed up the colonial educational *cursus honorum* all the way to further education in Senegal, the heart of the AOF. During this period, which partly coincided with the First World War, Houphouët was increasingly sucked into the colonial order.

The strain of the so-called Great War caused the first cracks in the European empires. But rather than

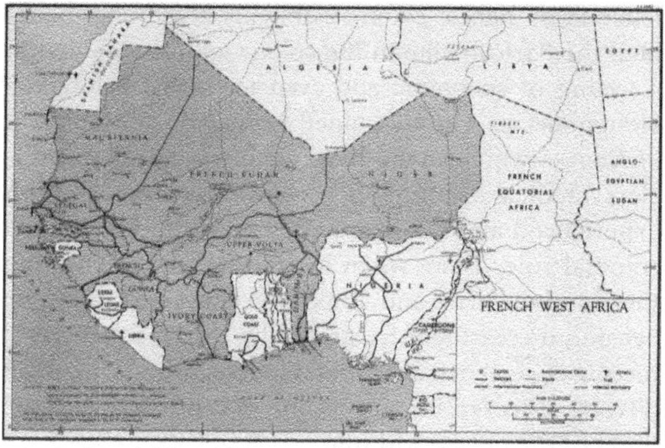

MAP 1.1. French West Africa, 1949. Courtesy of the National Archives Catalog.

leading to a questioning of the imperial project, the disproportionate contributions of the colonies in terms of manpower, raw materials, and strategic bases only whetted the appetite of the metropoles. Any nascent opposition was nipped in the bud, and thanks to the dismantlement of the German and Ottoman empires, the remaining European imperial powers were even able to expand their colonial portfolios. The interwar years thus saw the apogee of European imperialism. In the case of France, the contribution of its African colonies in the First World War had been particularly significant. This was the case for Côte d'Ivoire, which contributed the AOF's largest contingent of "volunteers" for France's war machine. Despite this sacrifice, the colony was relatively neglected and far from rivaling Senegal in French West Africa immediately after the war.

This was bound to change, however. With the promotion of such export crops as cocoa and coffee in the 1920s, Côte d'Ivoire advanced to become one of the federation's richest colonies. Initially, this boom benefited the African elite in the colony and contributed to a feeling of economic and even territorial belonging. Houphouët, as a newly trained African doctor (*médecin africain*)—which made him, on the basis of second-class medical training, a second-class doctor—both experienced and witnessed the inequalities of French colonial rule. Then, when he transitioned to running the family's farm and took over its chieftaincy, he became increasingly frustrated by the unequal treatment between African and French farmers in Côte d'Ivoire. This sentiment was only accentuated with the onset of the next world war.

In the wake of France's defeat at the hands of Nazi Germany in 1940, the colonial government of Côte d'Ivoire sided, along with the rest of the AOF, with the collaborationist French Vichy regime of Marshal Philippe Pétain. This led to an increasingly authoritarian colonialism and further economic exactions and difficulties and, concomitantly, even greater discrimination against Ivorians. Although the colony's switch to General Charles de Gaulle's Free French in 1943 brought some relief to Africans in Côte d'Ivoire, they nevertheless continued to make a disproportionate contribution to France's war effort, including by fighting in the ranks. It was in this setting, after having suffered under the pro-Vichy colonial regime, that Houphouët established and led the African Agricultural Union (Syndicat agricole africain, SAA) in 1944 to challenge the discriminatory colonial practices against African farmers. Then, when Paris opened the French parliament to a degree of colonial representation in the wake of the Second World War and in the spirit of the Brazzaville Conference,[1] which had recognized the key role of the colonies in France's survival, Houphouët seized the opportunity and became one of Côte d'Ivoire's representatives in the metropole. It was there that he made his breakthrough in the French Union—the postwar rebranding of France's empire—which then allowed him to bring together leading African politicians of French West Africa under the banner of the African Democratic Rally (Rassemblement démocratique africain, RDA).

In order to show how the Baoulé Dia Houphouët became the African leader Félix Houphouët-Boigny during the upheavals of the first half of the twentieth century, this chapter will discuss his childhood and education, medical role and experience, move to farming and unionism, and breakthrough in Ivorian and imperial politics.

Colonized Tradition

The first years of the life of the future Ivorian leader are the most steeped in legend. This is not necessarily surprising, because there was no or only a lacunary colonial record, and despite mythologized claims to the contrary, his destiny could not be known. In reconstructing his birth and early years, historians have had to draw on a combination of limited documentary evidence from his initial encounters with the colonial system and oral accounts whose transmission poses challenges familiar to many contexts beyond Africa. The information then increases in line with his educational progression, and it can be observed how his upbringing in Baoulé society became increasingly shaped by colonial influences.

The future leader of Côte d'Ivoire was born on 18 October 1905. This is at least the date of birth that was put forward by the Ivorian regime during his lifetime and was accepted as such by his hagiographers. Although the date has since been questioned and remains impossible to verify because of a lack of documentation, it can be assumed that he was at least born in the first decade of the twentieth century, most likely somewhere in the middle of it. His father, Ndoli Houphouët, originally from the surroundings of Didiévi in central Côte d'Ivoire, met his mother, Kimou N'Dri Kan, farther south in Kimoukro, a village founded by her father. Dia Houphouët was born from this union and, thanks to his mother, into Baoulé nobility. Yet his birth was apparently not appreciated, at least not by his father. It seems that as the third of four siblings—rather than the five of the official narrative—he supposedly disturbed the natural Baoulé order of three successive children of the same sex by being born after two girls. Within the tradition of his father's family, this required the killing of the troublemaker. But in a twist of luck, according to this story, baby Houphouët was saved from an early death by his mother and her family, who hailed from the Akouès, who had given up on this tradition. He was thus removed from the deadly clutches of his father and brought to safety in the small hamlet N'Gokro, where he would grow up under the protection of his great-aunt Yaa N'So. If this story is true, then knowing how close he had come to an early death could potentially have contributed to the future Ivorian leader's sense of insecurity.

Once in N'Gokro, however, Dia Houphouët lived a sheltered and relatively privileged early childhood under the care of his great-aunt. With no male heir of age available to govern, Yaa N'So was in charge of the village, which would be renamed Yamoussoukro in her honor. An adroit diplomat between the French colonizers and Akoué resisters, she came to be respected by her people and appreciated by the French. Open to outside influence, she apparently wanted her nephew Kouassi N'Go and great-nephew Houphouët, as part of their training to take over the chiefdom after her, to learn from the French to strengthen and transform their own society. As a result, Houphouët came into contact with the French from a very young age, and by the time his aunt died in 1909 they had already made a lasting impression on him. With Yaa N'So gone, Kouassi N'Go took over, but soon thereafter he was killed by Akoué resistance fighters as a result of his collaboration with the French. This left Houphouët as the next heir of the chiefdom. Too young to take over, however, the position of chief was temporarily given to his stepfather, Brou Diby, whom his mother had married after his father's early death.

By the time of these successive leadership changes in Yamoussoukro, Houphouët had already been enrolled in school, first in neighboring Bonzi and then in his own village, where elementary education was provided by the French station chief himself. The colonial school system formed an integral part of France's imperial project. While an important tool of colonial control, it also provided a space for negotiation and rapprochement between colonizer and colonized. At the elementary level, in addition to receiving a rudimentary education, the future chief and farmer also had to do humbling domestic work and gained basic training in agriculture. After five years, this "village school" education was completed, and he was the only pupil of the school in Yamoussoukro to be selected for attending the Central School Group of Bingerville in 1915. Bringing together the best pupils from across the colony, it was the most prestigious school in Côte d'Ivoire and created by the

French as an incubator for the Ivorian elite in the service of France. It was also during this time that he converted to Christianity and when baptized took the first name Félix. Although not necessarily an exceptional student, thanks to hard work he nevertheless managed to graduate first in his year. This allowed him to continue his educational journey outside of Côte d'Ivoire at the federal school of the AOF, William Ponty, in Senegal.

Situated at the time on Gorée Island outside of Dakar, the École Normale (Normal School) William Ponty was named after a former governor-general of the AOF and had originally been established in Saint-Louis in 1903. As its name indicates, the school's prime mission and specialization was in the training of teachers. The African teachers it produced formed an emerging intellectual elite that came to occupy an intermediate and mediating position between the colonial administration and the African population. By the time Houphouët entered the school, they had become a crucial cogwheel in the French colonial and administrative system. Yet this institution of higher education was so much more than a teacher training college, notwithstanding the key colonial function of teachers. It was where the French trained the AOF's African elite to help them effectively run this part of their empire and where, as a corollary, studied many of the future leaders of independent francophone West Africa. In addition to Houphouët, other prominent alumni of the school were, for instance, his future regional political allies and rivals Modibo Keïta from Mali, Hubert Maga from Dahomey, Hamani Diori from Niger, and Mamadou Dia from Senegal. Steeped in France's colonial tradition and mission, the École Normale provided an education over three years, leading towards a specialization in teaching, colonial administration, or medicine, particularly the preparation for the entrance examination to attend medical school. The future Ivorian leader chose this third option. Why he did so is not clear. The explanations are varied and range from the influence of a professor to an omen. In any case, following William Ponty and a successful entrance examination, he enrolled in the Medical School of the AOF in Dakar. This school, which also had sections for pharmacy and midwifery, did not provide a full medical training comparable to that in metropolitan France. Instead, in patronizing and colonialist fashion, students first had to follow general courses in such disciplines as physics, chemistry, and natural history, and thereafter received only a relatively rudimentary training in medicine to become "auxiliary," instead of fully-fledged, doctors.

Graduating first in his class of thirteen students, Félix Houphouët became an "indigenous auxiliary doctor" on 20 October 1925. He had thus climbed up through the colonizer's educational ladder of advancement from his village in Côte d'Ivoire to the federation's capital, Dakar. By the mid-1920s, he was therefore a product of the French colonial system, elevated to the African elite, but kept below the colonizer—both in terms of training and status. Culturally, he was increasingly "assimilated," notably through his conversion to Christianity. Nevertheless, the cultural environment of his childhood, with its spiritual practices and beliefs, had left its mark, and he continued to believe in omens, particularly in the one foretelling his destiny as a doctor.

African Doctor

In his late recollections of his time as an African doctor, Houphouët-Boigny presented his younger self as a man who had taken the fight to the colonialists to improve the life of fellow Africans. In combating alcoholism among the indigenous population, he recalled provoking "indignation among the Europeans" for "practically accusing them of genocide."[2] In his different medical postings, the future leader of Côte d'Ivoire seems indeed to have worked towards the improvement of the health and living conditions of his compatriots. This was not a sacrificial endeavor, however, and he simultaneously built his life and eventually veered towards his personal interests as a future farmer and chief.

Houphouët was very young when he embarked on his medical career. If his official birthday is taken as a reference point, he was twenty years old at his first posting. In any case, he certainly was in his early twenties when he arrived as a freshly trained auxiliary doctor at the hospital in Abidjan in December 1925. It was in this hospital, which was still under construction at the time of his arrival, that he received his practical medical training and gained his first experience in treating patients under the critical eyes of French doctors. The head of the hospital, Dr. Louis Bouffard, clearly distinguished and imposed a hierarchy between doctors educated in France and African doctors like Houphouët who had received only an incomplete medical education. Consequently, Houphouët learned the ropes of practicing medicine within the confines of what an auxiliary doctor was supposed to do, namely, caring for the sick, preparing medication, administering vaccinations, promoting hygiene, sanitation, and medical prevention, and screening for and detecting epidemic and social diseases. The young African doctor learned and completed these tasks to the satisfaction of Bouffard, who, despite his hierarchical and racially motivated thinking, warmly praised Houphouët in his evaluation. The working relationship with Bouffard's deputy was not, however, as positive and certainly not as cordial. Apparently, Dr. Henry not only bullied him when the more even-handed head of the hospital was absent, but also was instrumental in dispatching the auxiliary doctor to the far west of the country.

Whether Henry had a hand in the new posting or it was standard that after learning the ropes in Abidjan the African doctor was supposed to help fellow Ivorians in the countryside and thereby spread the gospel of French medicine, Houphouët was transferred in April 1927 to take over the medical position at the military post in Guiglo. There, as the sole doctor, he was in charge, and he only had to answer to the commander of the *cercle,* a small colonial administrative unit which consisted of cantons that in turn were made up of villages. The French officer in command was Captain Henry, who coincidentally had the same surname as Houphouët's supposed detractor in Abidjan but was favorably disposed towards the young African doctor. In his reports, which came to be endorsed by the French governor of Côte d'Ivoire himself, he praised Houphouët for his efforts both in the treatment of patients and in medical prevention, notably by trying to win over the population to vaccinating their children and following hygienic and sanitary instructions. Benefiting from a good working relationship with the commander, Houphouët seemed at ease in his role and made himself comfortable in Guiglo by having his own house built with family funds. This supposed idyllic situation was not to last, however, and a little more than two years after his arrival he received news, while on leave in Yamoussoukro, of a new posting.

Houphouët arrived at his new post, which was in Abengourou, by late 1929. It was there, in eastern Côte d'Ivoire and close to the border with Ghana, that he began not only tentatively and probably unconsciously his apprenticeship in politics, but also the transition into his future life as an influential African farmer and unionist. Moreover, it was where he started, despite quite some local animosity, a family. Yet first he had to settle into what he proudly considered to be a post reserved for European doctors, as opposed to supposedly less important African ones. While there probably was no such distinction in light of the scarcity of doctors in the colony, Abengourou certainly represented a step up from Guiglo on the colonial ladder. Houphouët fulfilled this supposedly more prestigious role to the satisfaction of both the local French administrator, François Raoul, and the head of Côte d'Ivoire's health service, Commander Dubalen, who was also a doctor. Based on Raoul's report, Dubalen highlighted that the African doctor was loved by indigenous and European populations alike. This was to change, however.

After a year into his post, Houphouët had identified alcohol as the biggest threat to the people of Abengourou. Confronted with apparently rampant alcoholism among the local Agni population, he lambasted them for their deadly habit while simultaneously criticizing their European suppliers. Instead of any dramatic change in behavioral patterns, this crusade against alcoholism brought him the animosity of the Agni and their European suppliers. While the former branded him a killjoy, the latter, fearing for their effortlessly lucrative business, mobilized the colonial administration, which eventually issued a warning against him. Although the 1930s witnessed the emergence of a public sphere in the

AOF, wherein African elites began to express political and cultural ideas, it was more tightly controlled and smaller than in the neighboring British colonies. It was also more pronounced in colonial and urban centers than in the Ivorian periphery, where Houphouët found himself.

The most significant and potentially harmful animosity he encountered, however, had its roots at the private level. The issue in question was his marriage, which led the French administrator of Abengourou to recommend in June 1931 that the young doctor be moved to another region. Against seemingly overwhelming odds, Houphouët had managed to win over and eventually marry the Ivorian Senegalese Khady Sow. The problem was that both sides of her family were anything but well disposed towards him. Her father, the rich Senegalese merchant and French citizen Aly Sow, could not fathom that his daughter would marry a subject, rather than a citizen, of France. On the mother's side, there was a two-layered problem. Not only was he a Baoulé and not an Agni, but his social standing was well below that of her daughter, who happened to be the niece of the regional king, Boa Kouassi. This dual ethnic and social affront did not further endear him to the local population, which was already displeased by his initiatives against alcoholism. Yet this animosity proved insufficient for the colonial government to heed the local administrator's advice to redeploy Houphouët to another region, and for him to refrain from embarking on another crusade.

Foreshadowing the next chapter of his career, and probably through his younger brother Augustin Djaha Kan, who was in charge of the family farm back home, he began to take an interest in the destiny of African farming. In Abengourou he witnessed firsthand the unfair treatment of African farmers, especially by European farmers and traders who bought their produce at a fixed, below-market price and sold it at much higher prices. After apparently first voicing his frustration with the status quo in writing, Houphouët received positive personal feedback for his cause from Governor Maurice Léon Bourgine himself, moving the doctor into action. In early 1933, he toured the region tirelessly to convince farmers to refuse to sell their produce at too low a price. By April, these efforts had led to the first strike to sell cocoa Côte d'Ivoire had ever seen. This was an ephemeral success, however. The strike had to be called off because of half-hearted support from the local colonial administration and because the African farmers faced potential ruin with the unsold cocoa about to perish. Exhausted from this tussle, and after having been at his post in Abengourou for three years straight, Houphouët requested a long break back home, which was granted.

But the three months he spent in Yamoussoukro failed to reinvigorate him. Instead, he returned to Abengourou with a strong desire to leave as soon as possible the place where he had encountered so much private and local animosity, as well as apparent political failure. The colonial administration was willing to grant his request for a transfer but, increasingly considering him a troublemaker, wanted to send him off to the Bouna region in the very north of Côte d'Ivoire. Confronted with this option, Houphouët apparently threatened to resign, which then led the governor to permit him to suggest and ultimately choose his next posting. He opted for Dimbokro, which, at close proximity to Yamoussoukro, allowed him to practice medicine and, especially, to bring up the two sons who had already been born from his marriage in Abengourou—Félix and Augustin—in his own culture and language. The presence among his kin first seemed to provide him with a renewed sense of mission as a doctor, but then eventually estranged him from the medical profession by bringing him fully into family affairs and local politics.

Upon his arrival in Dimbokro in 1934, the medical challenge he was confronted with was twofold. First, the medical infrastructure was extremely limited and thus needed to be built up. Second, and perhaps more importantly, he faced the task of guiding the local population from existing spiritual healing practices towards Western medical approaches. In this dual undertaking, Houphouët had the good fortune to benefit from the support of the new head of the Ivorian health service, Colonel Dr. Paul Botreau-Roussel, who embarked on a vast program to promote Western medicine by building up the medical infrastructure in Côte d'Ivoire. Simultaneously, Houphouët could count on the local political help of his brother Augustin, who in summer 1933 had taken over the mantle of cantonal chief following the passing of their mother's second husband. This combined support allowed Houphouët to transform Dimbokro into a fully functioning medical post with even an operating block. While this achievement earned him praise from his superiors, they soon noticed that he became ever less dedicated to his role as an African doctor.

Despite being officially in post in Dimbokro, Houphouët increasingly began to stand out not for his dedication to patients, but for his long absences and time spent with his family while looking after its interests in Yamoussoukro. Although his younger brother was in charge of the chieftaincy, Houphouët was the head of the family, and this role became more pronounced following the passing of his mother during this period.

Moreover, his heart and financial interests seemed to have irreversibly shifted from medicine to agriculture. Seeing better economic prospects in farming and, through his experience in Abengourou, the potential to improve the condition of African farmers, he teamed up with his brother in running the family farm while also engaging in unionism. By 1938, his superiors in the colonial service observed that it was time for him to make a choice between medicine and politics. His brother's death in late 1938 made that decision much simpler. Houphouët took over the family farm, dedicating himself more fully to agriculture, and by summer 1939, he was installed as the chief of the canton of the Akouès.

African Agricultural Union

In 1944, the year of the creation of the African Agricultural Union (Syndicat agricole africain, SAA), a French planter apparently mocked Houphouët by implying that expecting equal pay for his coffee was foolish.[3] This particular French self-confidence was unjustified in the end because the SAA eventually succeeded in putting the African farmers on an equal footing with the French ones. The agricultural union's significance, however, went well beyond equality in farming. It provided the basis for the struggle for African emancipation in Côte d'Ivoire and African liberation in francophone Africa, and it set a process in motion that would propel Houphouët from his chieftaincy to the forefront of Ivorian and regional politics. In Côte d'Ivoire itself, and in the words of the historian and future nemesis of Houphouëtism Laurent Gbagbo, "the biggest beneficiary" of these travails was not the Ivorian people but the "agrarian bourgeoisie."[4] Whether or not one agrees with this Marxist historical interpretation, it seems evident that as Côte d'Ivoire's largest landowner in 1939, Houphouët waged his fight against inequality and for African emancipation at least initially and to some extent out of self-interest.

Houphouët's initial political credibility among his peers came from not only his vast plantations but also his role as the chief of the canton of the Akouès. Theoretically, as the elder brother, he, rather than Augustin, should have succeeded their stepfather in the role of chief in 1933. But at the time, in pursuit of his medical career, Houphouët had generously ceded his place to his younger brother. Yet this apparent generosity was not necessarily that voluntary. There had supposedly been pressure from the colonial administration for him to refuse, because rather than an enforcer of French authority, he had been seen as a potential challenger. In 1939, such concerns did not seem to have been decisive, and with the chieftaincy rightfully his, he eventually acceded to this role. With the canton consisting of a grouping of villages, he found himself above village chiefs but had to answer to the French commander of the cercle. Appointed by the governor of Côte d'Ivoire, Houphouët was therefore, despite the limited and partly constructed nature of his chiefly authority under colonial rule, tasked with helping administer the canton, maintain discipline among village chiefs, and collect taxes for France. For as long as he fulfilled these "essential" roles, he was largely left to his own devices and could pursue his own priorities for the canton, which in his case and in line with his past occupation were the promotion of hygiene and other prophylactic measures. Yet more importantly, he could dedicate himself to farming, for it was as planter that Houphouët henceforth identified himself.

Since the early 1930s, Augustin—assisted by his elder brother Félix—had transformed the vast land holdings they had inherited into one of the largest plantations in Côte d'Ivoire by expanding the land utilized and the crops planted. When Houphouët formally took over this major enterprise after the passing of his brother, he had an appetite for more. Consequently, he initially dedicated the bulk of his energy to overseeing and further developing the farm and, in so doing, did not hesitate to take advantage of the powers of his chieftaincy, notably when it came to the allocation of the workforce by the colonial administration.

Before the Second World War, unlike after, he was not concerned by the destiny of this workforce, which largely consisted of forced laborers. Rather, he was concerned by the unequal distribution of this labor force between European and African farmers, and by the inequality between these two groups of planters more generally. With the dramatic agricultural expansion that Côte d'Ivoire witnessed during the interwar period, which transformed the colony from colonial backwater to asset, workers had become a contested resource. Although these forced laborers were increasingly scarce, they received harsh treatment from the French farmers, who were privileged in their allocation. But instead of the suffering of fellow Ivorians, it was the preferential treatment of European planters that irked Houphouët. The escalating exploitation and inequality by the Vichy administration during the Second World War then moved him and fellow African planters into action. Somewhat paradoxically, not only did the conflict's impact on Côte d'Ivoire provide them with new motivations, but the simultaneous occasional disruptions of metropolitan oversight also created moments of greater space for discussion and criticism of the colonial regime.

Ivorian farmers like Houphouët, together with such professionals as teachers, lawyers, and doctors, formed an African elite in the colony. Although the French had wanted, through their education policies, to create such an elite to serve their empire, its members were increasingly less willing to suffer unequal treatment at the hands of the colonialists. Within this elite, the Ivorian planters clearly stood out because they had the potential to rival their European counterparts. Then the imposition of a colonial administration by the Nazi-collaborationist Vichy regime pushed them over the edge. Pursuing a repressive and racialized agenda, the government of Marshal Philippe Pétain reversed the reforms of the 1930s Popular Front (a left-wing coalition government), reinstated the arbitrary *indigénat* (native code) of laws and regulations that assigned Africans an inferior legal status, expanded forced labor, and institutionalized racial segregation. Colonial administration, meanwhile, excluded educated Africans and instead relied on chiefs for local enforcement. Labor and crop requisitions became increasingly extensive and intrusive, leading to famine and exhaustion. Censorship, surveillance, and repression sought to quell dissent, while paternalist propaganda aimed to coax Africans into loyalty and voluntary submission to the deeply racialized colonial order.

Racism had always been part and parcel of French colonialism. With Vichy's policies and governors in charge, however, it became increasingly unhinged. Assisted by petty colonialists, the colonial administration attempted to segregate Ivorian society, and even such "assimilated" Africans and chiefs as Houphouët had to suffer blatantly racist insults. What seems to have infuriated him and his fellow African planters even more, though, was the further escalation of already discriminatory and exploitative farming policies. African planters, in contrast to their European counterparts, were constrained in the exploitation of their arable land, prevented from expanding their plantations, given very limited access to forced labor, if any, and controlled in the selling of their produce. Confronted with this situation, Houphouët and his fellow African planters were also painfully aware that their membership in the Agricultural Union of Côte d'Ivoire (Syndicat agricole de Côte d'Ivoire)—which, though a mixed organization, catered only to the interests of French farmers—was to no avail. Consequently, and in light of their relative economic weight, they moved towards establishing their own union with the help of other sections of the Ivorian elite. In this undertaking, they were fortunate to benefit from the reversal of the military situation in the Second World War, the demise of Vichy, and the—albeit somewhat limited—acknowledgment by the Free French that they owed their survival in large part to France's African colonies.

Inasmuch as conditions in Côte d'Ivoire did not change overnight with the Free French takeover of the administration in 1943, the Brazzaville Conference of 1944 was not necessarily the watershed in France's colonial policy, nor the beginning of French decolonization in Africa, that it has often been portrayed to be. Whereas de Gaulle's lieutenants claimed to serve the ideal of liberty, many of Vichy's coercive colonial practices remained in place, including forced labor and repression. The conference convened by de Gaulle in Brazzaville in 1944 was similarly contradictory. On the one hand, it was intended as a new dawn in France's African empire and to portray Free France as both liberal and democratic.

On the other hand, it was an entirely French affair to which no Africans were invited and where decolonization was ruled out. Instead, France's sovereignty was supposed to be retained within a restructured empire based on association that allowed only for limited African representation and made vague promises for gradual social, educational, and labor reforms. It was to some extent a propagandistic exercise that was aimed at showing Free France's moral superiority over Vichy and reinvigorating the French empire while the past practices of racial hierarchy, paternalism, and authoritarian control were maintained. Despite these obvious shortcomings, Brazzaville's rhetoric of reform galvanized African political mobilization, and the Gaullist takeover of France's African colonies, notably in Côte d'Ivoire, put a different kind of colonial administrator in charge.

After assuming control from Vichy in 1943, the Free French sent a governor to Côte d'Ivoire who had an open ear for African demands for the colonial territory. This was particularly the case for Ivorian planters, not least because the reformist governor, André Latrille, realized that their unequal treatment was not only morally wrong, but also economically flawed because it limited agricultural production in Côte d'Ivoire and thus for the French empire. Although he was assailed by unrepentant French colonizers and planters who feared for their privileges, Latrille chose to support the African farmers in their quest for equal rights. As a result, by summer 1944 the SAA was born and recognized by the French colonial authorities with Houphouët as its president. The future Ivorian leader, according to his own portrayal, had been roped into this position because he was French educated, had long served as a doctor and thus civil servant, and held a chiefly title. Consequently, he had the necessary understanding, connections, and authority for the role. Initially though, he had apparently refused to take on this part, as his "only ambition was to devote [himself] to the affairs of [his] small canton" after having lost not only his mother and brother but also his eldest son, Félix.[5] This narrative can, however, be attributed to a certain false humility because it is more likely that he played a central role in the creation of the SAA, and it was thus only logical that he would become its president.

At least once the SAA was established, Houphouët was undisputably a driving force and contributed to its success. In cooperation with Governor Latrille, he and his colleagues managed to gradually remove the discriminations against African planters, and this led to the union's appeal and rapid growth from five thousand to twenty thousand members. In going beyond merely a fight for equality, the SAA also created cooperatives for African farmers for selling their produce and buying the farming materials they needed at more favorable rates. But it was by taking on the issue of forced labor that Houphouët and his union lifted their struggle to new heights. Facing escalating opposition and lobbying against him from European planters, and fighting a cause that was not confined to Côte d'Ivoire, the future Ivorian leader embarked on a path that would lead him to Paris and propel him to the forefront of regional politics.

Political Breakthrough

The SAA provided Houphouët with an ideal springboard to a successful political career. According to Denise Gadeau, a secretary of his at the time, when the agricultural union became involved in politics in

1945, its leader was an omnipresent force in its headquarters and "buzzing with ideas."[6] This personal drive and effective organization would not have been sufficient, however, without the opportunities the changed imperial landscape presented. In line with the "spirit of Brazzaville," France's postwar leaders were aware that they could not just carry on with business as usual. In addition to owing a "moral" debt to the empire and, especially, the African colonies for keeping the Free French on life support and eventually helping to save France, the imperial enterprise had been discredited more broadly. Alongside anti-colonial pressure from the emerging superpowers—the United States and the Soviet Union—Europe's colonial powers had shown through military defeats, particularly in Asia, that they were not invincible. While the First World War might have caused some minor cracks to imperial edifices, the Second World War opened up a space for anti-colonial contestation in the colonies and led to a realization in the metropoles that reform was necessary.

In the case of France, where politicians, irrespective of their political affiliation, wanted to cling on to the empire, the solution was supposed to be a French union that would give the colonized a moderate yet manageable voice. Consequently, in the elections for the French Constituent National Assembly of 1945, a limited number of seats were allocated for Africans. This provided Houphouët with the unique opportunity to make a political breakthrough or, rather, rapidly succeeding breakthroughs.

Houphouët was, in his own words, "solicited from all sides to present himself in the second college" for the elections of the Constituent National Assembly in autumn 1945.[7] While the "first college" allowed only French citizens to present themselves, the second one was open to French "subjects" like Houphouët, who was an obvious choice as the SAA president and seems to have not needed much convincing to present himself. In his election campaign, he could draw on his status and network as a local chief, his substantial wealth, and, above all, the machinery of his agricultural union, which he skillfully used to great effect to win over constituencies and sideline potential opponents. While he tried to parry accusations that he was anti-French by professing his loyalty to Paris, the key elements of his electoral program were equal political rights for all Ivorians and the abolition of forced labor. In addition, he wanted to expand education and, in line with his past occupation, promote health and medical services.

These ways and means proved to be successful, and in late October he was elected with 12,680 votes, a majority of almost 3,000. This majority shrank to a little more than 1,000 in the second ballot of November, which was held because of an apparent irregularity in the first one. Nevertheless, he was clearly elected, and in early December he left Abidjan for Paris. On his way, he announced the yet to be fully explained decision, which according to Paul-Henri Siriex was to meet France's civil status regulations,[8] to add a matronymic to his name: Boigny, which could be traced back to his maternal ancestor and the founder of Yamoussoukro, Boigny N'Dri, and symbolized a ram and its strength and determination. By the end of 1945, he thus arrived in the capital of the French empire as Félix Houphouët-Boigny.

The leading Ivorian planter formally took his seat as a deputy in the Constituent Assembly on 5 February 1946, and about a month later he joined the parliamentary group led by the French Communist Party (Parti communiste français, PCF). The reason for joining this particular group, according to a narrative later propagated by Houphouët-Boigny himself, was his idea to distribute the African deputies into as many different parliamentary groups as possible to increase their political leverage. Consequently, while others were affiliated to such groups as that of the French Section of the Workers' International (Section française de l'Internationale ouvrière, SFIO), he joined the communists. More likely reasons why he and a number of African deputies ended up in this group, however, were that the communists, who held the most seats in the assembly, actively wooed them by supporting their emancipatory policies. This was notably the case for the abolition of forced labor, which would propel Houphouët-Boigny into the political limelight as a champion for African rights. Continuing a battle he had begun in Côte d'Ivoire, and working together with other deputies, he took the lead on a bill for the abolition of forced labor in France's overseas territories. Following prior interventions to prepare the ground, he formally advocated for the bill to the assembly on two occasions in late March. Presaging his future policies at the helm of Côte d'Ivoire, he made his case for the abolition of forced labor by insisting on his respect for France and, in laying out his economic rationale, his experience as a major planter and leader of the SAA:

> It is as free men that we intend to freely enter the French Union. But we are not all free. The forced labor to which we are still subjected, this remnant of the corvée so decried in France, will make us slaves in the Union if it is not abolished first. In the French Union there cannot be masters and slaves, but elders and younger members of the same great family, younger members respectful

of age and grateful for services rendered, elders anxious to help the younger members catch up with them on the difficult road to freedom and civilization. . . . Plantations can also survive the radical and immediate abolition of forced labor. It is not . . . a demagogue speaking to you. It is a large landowner who has freely renounced forced labor, a man who lives exclusively from this exploitation with his large family, a man whom more than 12,000 of his peers have chosen to preside over the only large agricultural group existing in French Black Africa, a man who, if he were a demagogue, would risk plunging hundreds and hundreds of brave farmers who have placed all their trust in him into misery. We remain firmly convinced that if the colonists pay the laborers well and, above all, treat them better, they will not only maintain their production but even increase it.[9]

The assembly sided with the leading African planter against the colonists. The bill was voted through on 5 April 1946, and from that day forced labor was to be phased out and ultimately abolished. This was truly a triumph for Houphouët-Boigny. While he managed to strengthen the position of Ivorian farmers by liberating the labor force that had previously been commandeered by French planters, he also emerged as the great liberator of Africans from the bonds of slavery.

The successes of first his election as deputy, and then the abolition of forced labor, contributed significantly to the establishment of his party in Côte d'Ivoire and his emergence as a political leader in francophone Africa. Building on the momentum of the election campaign for the Constituent Assembly, the Democratic Party of Côte d'Ivoire (Parti démocratique de Côte d'Ivoire, PDCI) was formally established in April 1946, shortly after the "Houphouët-Boigny Law" for the abolition of forced labor had been passed. The party's base was the SAA, with its members and supporters, as well as its financial, organizational, and logistical resources. But beyond this core, the PDCI also reached out to and relied on professionals, salaried workers, unions, ethnic organizations, communist study groups, and cultural associations, transforming the party into a genuine mass movement. This enabled it to move beyond the African farming lobby, transcend local and ethnic divisions, become a national force, and rapidly grow from 40,000 to over 270,000 members within a year. In combination with its leader's popularity, the PDCI thus came to eclipse its rivals, the SFIO's Ivorian branch and the Progressive Party of Côte d'Ivoire (Parti progressiste de Côte d'Ivoire). The elections for the second Constituent Assembly in May 1946 were therefore a mere formality, and Houphouët-Boigny was elected with 23,271 votes out of a total of 23,994.

Back in Paris by late spring 1946, Houphouët-Boigny first focused on a relatively small yet tangible project: scholarships for Ivorian pupils to enable them to study in France. Although the Ministry of the Colonies approved them, it only did so because their cost was covered by the SAA. Nevertheless, it allowed 150 Ivorian pupils to study in France, and among them was a certain Marie-Thérèse Brou, who would one day become his second wife. Yet this was still well in the future, and in the meantime, he continued his struggle for equality in the French Union in parliament.

Vociferous in his criticism of colonists but without ever considering rejecting France, he called for a relationship of equals between French and Africans, and the metropole and the colonies. But his hopes, and those of other African deputies, were disappointed. With French policymakers and legislators increasingly withdrawing from the "spirit of Brazzaville," the thinking of the African deputies began to go beyond both their individual territories and the French assembly.

In order to increase their political leverage in favor of equality, they began to organize themselves, with Houphouët-Boigny leading on the idea to galvanize their supporters by uniting their forces during a meeting back in Africa, in Bamako. Although initially in favor of the idea, such senior African deputies as the Senegalese Amadou Lamine Guèye—who had taught the young Houphouët mathematics at William Ponty—and Léopold Sédar Senghor—the famous poet and future president of Senegal—eventually withdrew their support. Their resulting absence at the meeting in Bamako was supposedly because of machinations by the colonial government and the SFIO, the party with which these leaders were affiliated in Paris. While the socialists were certainly critical of them working with PCF-affiliated African deputies, it was also that their assimilationist and reformist positions clashed with Houphouët-Boigny's more radical ideas and confrontational approach.

Nevertheless, the meeting in the capital of French Sudan (future Mali) in mid-October 1946 brought together a whole range of African leaders, many of whom would later play key roles in the destiny of their territories, namely, for instance, Ahmed Sékou Touré of Guinea, Hamani Diori of Niger, Émile Derlin Zinsou of Dahomey, and Modibo Keïta of the French Sudan itself. Committed to make their voices heard throughout the region and in Paris, those present established the African

Democratic Rally (Rassemblement démocratique africain, RDA) as a federation of political parties in francophone Africa. As a result, Houphouët-Boigny's party in Côte d'Ivoire, for instance, became the PDCI-RDA. More significantly, he himself emerged as the formal leader of this transnational political movement. In addition to his key role in the RDA's establishment and anticolonial credentials from the abolition of forced labor, he benefited from the leadership vacuum created by the boycott of the conference by his political elders, particularly those from Senegal.

In the wake of Bamako, Houphouët-Boigny was riding an ever-growing political wave. Following the establishment of the French Fourth Republic in autumn 1946, he and his party clearly dominated the elections in Côte d'Ivoire, and his movement extended its influence throughout the region. Consequently, when he returned to Paris for a third time—this time for a longer period of five years—he was already an extraordinary political figure who wielded influence throughout francophone Africa. He and his movement were, however, affiliated with the PCF, the only French party that had sent a delegate to Bamako. With the onset of the Cold War, and the emergence of an increasingly anti-communist mood in Paris, his wave would thus eventually be broken by the French government and colonial authorities.

2

African Nationalist *Malgré Lui*

> I waited for the fiancée on the square of the church with a bouquet in my hands. The fiancée did not come. The flowers wilted.
>
> —Félix Houphouët-Boigny, December 1959

With the rather colorful analogy from the above epigraph, Houphouët-Boigny voiced his disappointment and frustration at de Gaulle's acquiescence to the Mali Federation's demand for independence in late 1959, which sounded the death knell of the Ivorian leader's much-cherished French Community. He had been a strong advocate for this last formal association to salvage the French empire in Côte d'Ivoire, francophone Africa, and the world, for he had seen it as the key to his country's and his own prosperity. He had invested substantial political capital, and now, with his dream in tatters, he sought to reassert his standing as an African nationalist by challenging the general and pursuing outright independence without strings attached. The Ivorian leader was thus, as this episode illustrates particularly well, able to reinvent himself and pragmatically adapt to changed circumstances. While he was no stranger to confronting the French authorities, he had already shown political expediency by turning his coat in 1950. Faced with repression against the PDCI-RDA in Côte d'Ivoire and fearing for his own well-being, he had broken with the French communists and aligned himself with the political establishment in Paris.

Riding a wave of political success in 1946, Houphouët-Boigny probably would have found it hard to imagine that he would all of a sudden be faced with such hostility from the French colonial administration that he would feel the need to reinvent himself and his movement as one of its strongest allies. Despite temporary episodes of hostility in his earlier life, he seemed to succeed at everything—education, medicine, farming, and multiple levels of politics—rising from Baoulé nobility to lead the SAA, champion African rights in Paris, and build a transnational movement within the French empire.

Although the French Union was in essence a rebranding exercise for the French empire under the banner of the republican ideals of equality and association and lacked fundamental reforms, Houphouët-Boigny sought to work within and not against it. Like the Senegalese Léopold Sédar Senghor, he initially embraced reform within French institutions, and rather than to dismantle, he sought to transform the empire into a federal and egalitarian community. It was not about breaking with France but, with a focus on citizenship, about making Africans free and French within a pluralistic empire. Senghor, in line with his intellectual agenda of humanist Africanism (Négritude), envisioned a transnational democracy, realized through a federation linking Europe and Africa and based on sovereignty and cultural reciprocity. In contrast to his Senegalese colleague in the French parliament, Houphouët-Boigny did not have such a grand and intellectually grounded vision. Instead, and as illustrated by the case of forced labor, he relied on republican ideals as he pursued pragmatic reform to advance equality. He was nevertheless not devoid of federal ideals and could envisage a federation linking France and its colonies in the postwar period. But this vision was from the outset grounded in what he saw as Côte d'Ivoire's interests, and after his political realignment in the early 1950s, it increasingly centered on a direct federal link with Paris rather than with the other African colonies. At no point did Houphouët-Boigny wish to relinquish the French connection, and even when decolonization seemed inevitable, he, unlike Senghor, would cling to the French Community. Consequently, although by the late 1940s he came to be perceived as an imperial nemesis in Paris, he would certainly never have characterized himself as such. A hardworking and gifted politician, he had benefited from a reformed imperial and colonial environment, as well as support from the French communists, in his meteoric postwar rise. With the onset of the Cold War, however, the political environment deteriorated considerably, and the communist connection became a serious liability.

Whereas the Allied victory and French experience in the Second World War had led to imperial reforms, the outbreak of the Cold War, combined with colonial troubles in Indochina, Algeria, and Madagascar, provoked a more forceful policy vis-à-vis the colonies in Paris. While trying to hold on to imperial possessions in Southeast Asia, successive French postwar governments wanted to rely, in line with the logic of *Eurafrique*,[1] on African resources for reestablishing France as a power of the first rank. Consequently, they were not willing to tolerate challenges to their colonial authority, which they saw as increasingly threatened by the combined forces of communism and African nationalism.

After the PCF had been excluded from the French government in 1947, Houphouët-Boigny and his communist-affiliated party and movement thus came to be in the crosshairs of the colonial administration. Refusing to tone down its political discourse, demands, and activities, the PDCI-RDA faced escalating repression. This eventually led Houphouët-Boigny to change course, break with the communists, and align himself with the French political establishment. Once he had silenced the radical wing of his party and sold this solution to the Ivorian people, he worked in tandem with the colonial authorities, served in successive French governments, and influenced and championed reincarnations of the French empire. The first reincarnation passed the *loi-cadre* (framework law) of 1956, through which Paris gave the colonies more financial responsibility for economic and social development while remaining in charge of foreign affairs, defense, and monetary policy. The second one was, after de Gaulle's return to power in 1958, the French Community, which gave the colonies autonomy within a federal construct that was still to rely on France for its foreign policy and defense. And it was when the Community fell apart that Houphouët-Boigny would seek for outright independence.

This chapter will show how the Ivorian leader first fought against and suffered under the colonial comeback, then transformed into an ally and champion of French imperialism, and finally challenged de Gaulle's authority when bringing Côte d'Ivoire into the postcolonial age. Despite seemingly dramatic political turns, Houphouët-Boigny pragmatically adapted to evolving circumstances in pursuit of what he considered best for his territory and himself.

Imperial Nemesis

With his politics in Côte d'Ivoire and France in the wake of the Second World War, Houphouët-Boigny had made a great many enemies amongst the colonists in the colony and their lobby in the metropole. Meanwhile, his and the RDA's alliance with the communists had not gone unnoticed amongst the French political establishment. Following the Cold War–induced exclusion of the PCF from the governing coalitions in 1947, he and his movement thus found themselves without protection in the executive. More significantly, instead of a more progressive governor such as Latrille, in autumn 1948 Paris unleashed the archconservative Laurent Élisée Péchoux on Côte d'Ivoire with the PDCI-RDA as his target. Thus began the harassment by the police, which meant that party employees like Houphouët-Boigny's secretary Denise Gadeau "were searched every day."[2] But neither he nor his party was ready to cave in, and as a result, the situation escalated.

Houphouët-Boigny, an immensely wealthy planter and landowner, did nothing to alleviate French concerns that he was in cahoots with the communists—on the contrary. Writing in the Senegalese and RDA-affiliated publication *Réveil* (Awakening) in December 1947, he called on the socialist and communist elected officials to "present a united front" because they "would be doing a disservice to the working class . . . if they did not resist together the forces of reaction, [because] the reactionary colonial administration [was] promoting anti-communism overseas in order to set African democrats against one another."[3] This call for left-wing unity after the exclusion of the communists from the government showed an awareness that he and his movement were now up against the French government and colonial administration. Simultaneously, however, they were also emboldened by their own political strength, with the RDA having significant backing and electoral representation in the metropole, the region, and particularly Côte d'Ivoire. The PDCI-RDA and its supporters thus continued to build on its momentum by rallying Ivorians throughout the territory to its cause for equality between colonizer and colonized. But in its enthusiasm, the party also exposed itself to retributions from the colonial administration by usurping colonial regalian rights, going as far as to set up its own courts and police, influence local chiefs, and raise taxes in some parts of Côte d'Ivoire.

By clearly stepping on the prerogatives of the colonial administration, Houphouët-Boigny and his movement gave Governor Péchoux, in addition to political and ideological motivations, an actual reason to move against them. Once in post, he employed the full force of the law to dismantle the rival infrastructures they had put in place and to strengthen those of the colonial administration. Meanwhile, in order to politically weaken the PDCI-RDA, he supported existing political rivals and enabled the buildup of new ones—namely, the Progressive Party of Côte d'Ivoire, the Entente of Independents of Côte d'Ivoire, the Eburnean Democratic Bloc, and, a socialist himself, the SFIO's Ivorian branch. Moreover, in a more direct subversive attack against the broad church of the PDCI-RDA, he tried to deepen existing divisions, encourage dissent and disaffection, and eventually lure away dissidents. In combination with this political and psychological campaign, the governor also targeted Ivorian merchants and planters by allowing, for instance, a race to the bottom in the prices paid for their commodities. While these machinations began to have a significant corrosive effect on Houphouët-Boigny and his movement, matters came to a head in early 1949.

On 6 February in the Treichville neighborhood of Abidjan, PDCI-RDA supporters violently clashed with opposition members who had been encouraged, if not instructed, by Péchoux. This gave the governor the perfect excuse to ramp up his repression of Houphouët-Boigny's movement. While some were caught in the act, the colonial administration, holding the PDCI-RDA responsible for the violence, indiscriminately rounded up its members, all the way up to leadership, in the wake of the clash.

This was the beginning of a period of anxiety in Côte d'Ivoire that raised alarm bells in Paris and caused international consternation. In response to the arbitrariness and sheer scale of the arrests, as well as the seemingly open-ended preventive detention, the PDCI-RDA declared a series of strikes, some of the detainees went on hunger strikes, and their wives and hundreds of female supporters demonstrated in front of the colonial administration in Abidjan. Moreover, a crescendo of demonstrations by party members and supporters turned into riots and clashes with the colonial security forces, which led to increasing numbers of deaths and casualties on both sides, but predominantly among the PDCI-RDA. Many in the movement believed that the struggle and the resulting suffering were the price to pay for freedom.

Houphouët-Boigny himself, like a tribune of the people, rallied and motivated his troops through increasingly incendiary speeches—at least until the repression landed on his doorstep. With the colonial administration fearing further escalation and a colony-wide uprising orchestrated by Houphouët-Boigny, the prosecutor issued an arrest warrant against him in early 1950. When presented with the warrant by the deputy prosecutor, the RDA leader was so furious and caused such a stir that the former decided to withdraw to avoid a clash with the latter's supporters.

Ultimately though, it was because of his parliamentary immunity that Houphouët-Boigny avoided arrest. Moreover, as a deputy in the French National Assembly and with the support of fellow RDA representatives, he managed to call out the colonial abuses in Paris and help bring them to the attention of world opinion. Nevertheless, he increasingly feared not only for his movement's future, but also for his own. In addition to his close arrest, the government in Paris was moving towards outlawing the RDA in all of France's African colonies, and the mysterious death of Victor Biaka Boda—a PDCI-RDA senator in Paris—with the apparent involvement of colonial security forces, made him realize that no one was really safe. He thus concluded that he had to act to save his movement and skin, and therefore began the process of breaking with the communists and ingratiating himself with the French government.

Although he had apparently kept a strategic backchannel with AOF governor-general Paul Béchard since 1948, he began to put his plan in motion upon his return to Paris in spring 1950. Advised by Raphaël Saller, the senator of French Guinea, and through the intermediary of cabinet staffer Paul-Henri Siriex, he eventually met with the new president of the Council of Ministers,[4] René Pleven, in September. Houphouët-Boigny took this opportunity to convey to Pleven that he was now focused on supporting the French Union. This message seems to have resonated with the president of the council, because after the meeting he instructed the minister of overseas France to continue the conversation with the Ivorian leader. François Mitterrand and Houphouët-Boigny then sealed, despite mutual apprehensions, the deal: In exchange for breaking with the communists and throwing his weight behind the French Union, the RDA leader obtained from Paris an end to the repression of the (PDCI-)RDA, the release of political prisoners, and the recall of hostile colonial administrators.

While this deal between Mitterrand and Houphouët-Boigny brought much-needed relief to the movement under siege, breaking up with the long-term communist allies and going to bed with the enemy was hard, if not impossible, to digest for the more radical left of the RDA. Most prominently, Houphouët-Boigny clashed with Gabriel d'Arboussier, a cofounder of the movement and its secretary-general. The RDA leader eventually won this test of strength, obtained from d'Arboussier his resignation as secretary-general, and managed to carry the movement and party in Côte d'Ivoire with him. But his transition from imperial nemesis to imperial cheerleader came to many as a shock and still required a period of digestion and implementation.

Imperial Cheerleader

Houphouët-Boigny's realignment of his party in Côte d'Ivoire and movement in the region with the ruling parties in Paris, specifically Pleven's and Mitterrand's Democratic and Socialist Union of the Resistance (Union démocratique et socialiste de la Résistance, UDSR), did not fail to ruffle a few feathers and caused considerable consternation. In a testament to his authority in the PDCI-RDA and political acumen, however, he managed to sideline his most vociferous critics and take his support base into a new era of collaboration with the imperial power. Facilitated by this newfound partnership, he then managed to absorb the rival political organizations in Côte d'Ivoire into the PDCI-RDA, and thereby pave the way for one-party rule.

This contrasted with the Gold Coast's Kwame Nkrumah, who, rather than uniting, fragmented his Convention People's Party (CPP) during the 1950s. Yet this was not the only area of contrast with Nkrumah. Somewhat counter-cyclically, the Ivorian leader threw his full support behind France's efforts to cling to its empire in Africa, while his Ghanaian counterpart and future rival, as well as other West African leaders, fought for and moved their countries towards independence. Moreover, integrating successive governments of the volatile French Fourth Republic, Houphouët-Boigny helped shape imperial policies that, rather than strengthening francophone Africa, divided its colonial territories. In so doing, he inevitably clashed with his other regional rival, Senegal's Senghor, who favored a federal structure for France's African colonies. Favoring a direct link to Paris and seeing his and Côte d'Ivoire's success and prosperity better secured with than without France, Houphouët-Boigny continued to cheer on the French empire after de Gaulle's return to power in 1958. During the decade in which French imperialism came under increasing strain—with the loss of Indochina and the descent into the quagmire of Algeria—Africa began to attract the superpowers' attention, and the wave of African decolonization took shape; the Ivorian leader thus became a self-interested ally of French colonialism.

Initially, it was not clear how Houphouët-Boigny's political gamble would play out. In the wake of the RDA's formal political realignment, a substantial degree of bewilderment existed in the movement's ranks and among its supporters, particularly in Côte d'Ivoire. Despite visible backing from Mitterrand, the other political forces in the territory sensed an opportunity to take on the previously almighty PDCI-RDA. The first test came with the elections for the French National Assembly in June 1951, during which the party's political adversaries joined forces in rival electoral lists. The outcome offered both reassurance and warning to Houphouët-Boigny. Although his party emerged victorious from the contest with a sizable majority, it was not large enough to obtain both of Côte d'Ivoire's parliamentary seats. Instead of his friend Daniel Ouezzin Coulibaly, it was Sékou Sanogo, from the opposing French Union electoral list, who would represent the Ivorians with Houphouët-Boigny in Paris.

There, the Ivorian leader felt the need to explain his reversal first to fellow RDA politicians in private, and then to the assembly in public. Insisting on his aim to defend the general interests of all Africans within the French Union and in accordance with the law, he argued that the alliance with the communists had not been ideological, but a pure matter of political expediency that had now passed its sell-by date. This was also largely the script he followed when he finally chose to address his fellow Ivorians. Moreover, in making a virtue of necessity, in his speech at Abidjan's Géo André Stadium, he also extended his hand to his political opponents and the French colonialists in Côte d'Ivoire:

> The R.D.A. can do a lot in this country: it can and must bring together people of good will,

> regardless of their political ideology, to jointly achieve a program of economic and social progress in the best interests of Côte d'Ivoire, France, and the French Union. We realized that our alignment with the communist group was, to some extent, an obstacle to this rapprochement. . . . We have ended our association with the communist group. We have voted for and continue to express our trust in the governments. . . . We have never shared the communist ideology. But it is clear that our parliamentary action . . . would be in vain if, in a territory like Côte d'Ivoire, where the vast majority trusts us . . . , we did not succeed in collaborating with all those, White and Black, who, like us, have a primary interest in seeing this territory, with its infinite possibilities, resolutely embark on the path of economic and social progress.[5]

In extending his hand, he not only publicly repudiated communism, but also marked an end to the political struggle against the French authorities, choosing instead economic and social development in partnership with France. Supported by the French government, and notably the more friendly governors that succeeded Péchoux, his strategy proved successful.

With a return to stability in Côte d'Ivoire and the PDCI-RDA leadership firmly in the hands of moderates, other parties and politicians were willing to join forces with Houphouët-Boigny and his party. For the territorial elections of March 1952, the SFIO, the Independents, and a number of colonialists joined him and the PDCI-RDA in the Union for the Economic and Social Development of Côte d'Ivoire (Union pour le développement économique et social de la Côte d'Ivoire, UDESCI). This electoral coalition was a resounding success, and with a clear majority of the votes it secured twenty-eight out of fifty seats in the Territorial Assembly, which was henceforth to be presided over by none other than Houphouët-Boigny himself.

With his political fortunes recovering at such an astounding pace, in autumn 1952 he found the necessary time and headspace to regularize his private situation by marrying the twenty-five-years-younger Marie-Thérèse Brou to the detriment of Khady Sow, his first wife and the mother of their four surviving children. Although this second marriage did not have the blessing of the church, it was legally aboveboard and did not adversely impact his further political career and rise.

In the years immediately following his political recovery and second marriage, Houphouët-Boigny consolidated his positions in both Côte d'Ivoire and Paris, which mutually reinforced each other. With the colonial administration's backing, he advanced the economic and social development of the colony. The resulting stability and prosperity in turn benefited and was appreciated by the French government, which came to see the Ivorian leader as a major asset in its late imperial endeavors. This led, on the one hand, to his reelection for the French National Assembly in a landslide victory in the Ivorian elections of January 1956, with the second Ivorian seat going this time to his ally Daniel Ouezzin Coulibaly. Regionally, these elections were also a significant success for Houphouët-Boigny because they brought nine RDA representatives in total, including Guinea's Ahmed Sékou Touré, to Paris. On the other hand, and related to Houphouët-Boigny's regional, in addition to his territorial, strength, Prime Minister Guy

Mollet invited him in February to join the French cabinet as minister delegate to the Presidency of the Council. The same year, he ended up cumulating this function with yet another one that was not atypical for a member of the French cabinet—namely that of mayor, and in his case, of Abidjan.

Houphouët-Boigny's eyes and presence were, however, focused on Paris and imperial, rather than local, politics. Although in his ministerial role he was supposed to work on the French Union's constitutional reform, his input into what would become the *loi-cadre* was more indirect than direct, despite his claims to the contrary. Nevertheless, his influence was not negligible, and he was notably consulted by Overseas Minister Gaston Defferre during the elaboration of the bill.

Frustrated with the increasingly wealthy Côte d'Ivoire having to contribute more to the AOF than it received from it, the Ivorian leader took advantage of his position to strengthen the role of the individual colonies and to reduce the power of Dakar and Brazzaville, the capitals of the AOF and French Equatorial Africa (Afrique équatoriale française, AEF), respectively. In advocating for the transformation of these federations from executive into coordinating bodies, he attracted the ire of Senghor, the main proponent of the federal solution, whose territory had benefited from the previous constitutional framework and who had been Houphouët-Boigny's regional political rival since the creation of the RDA in 1946. During the debate of the bill in the National Assembly, the Senegalese leader did not mince his words in addressing the French government and its Ivorian minister: "You are balkanizing Africa, you are going against its aspiration for unity."[6] This criticism was justified, because rather than focusing on unity in francophone Africa, Houphouët-Boigny clearly prioritized Côte d'Ivoire. According to Pierre Messmer, the colony's governor at the time, the destruction of the AOF was Houphouët-Boigny's "main objective."[7] In response, Senghor tried to fight this position not only in Paris but also regionally. Yet while his efforts to create a federal movement encountered limited success, Houphouët-Boigny actually came to face some headwind from within his own movement, notably at the 1957 RDA congress in Bamako, where the majority did not share his anti-federal position.

Despite opposition from his regional francophone rivals and peers, the Ivorian leader continued his support for the *loi-cadre* and championed the reformed French Union, after the law had been passed in June 1956, as a member of successive iterations of the French government. This advocacy went across the linguistic divide in Africa and reached beyond the Atlantic. While hosting Nkrumah—now prime minister of the newly independent Ghana—in early April 1957, he showed off Abidjan's shiny new infrastructure by emphasizing that it had been made possible by France's generosity. Moreover, he threw down the gauntlet to the Ghanaian leader through the now famous wager that in ten years Côte d'Ivoire would, with French help, surpass independent Ghana in its economic and social development. No less self-confident, Nkrumah accepted the wager, and this was the beginning of one of decolonizing Africa's most significant rivalries. But more imminently, Ghana became Houphouët-Boigny's point of reference when he justified the French Union and France's continued imperial role in Africa to the American political establishment in a *Foreign Affairs* article in July 1957. In contrast "to the type of independence . . . of Ghana," he argued, the French Union provided the "conditions that are indispensable to the creation of an economic and social environment in which the African people can attain a standard of living comparable to that of the peoples of the great modern nations."[8]

Houphouët-Boigny made the case for Côte d'Ivoire's collaboration with France from an increasingly all-powerful domestic political position, because his approach to economic and social development not only resonated with the Ivorian electorate, but also benefited the country's elites. The political union he had been calling for thus became a reality. In May 1956, he led a rally at the Géo André Stadium in Abidjan, where he announced, in the presence of the other major Ivorian parties and their leaders, that their parties would fuse with his PDCI-RDA. By the end of the year, these parties had been dissolved and merged with, or rather absorbed by, Houphouët-Boigny's party.

In the territorial elections of March 1957, Ivorian politicians were thus jockeying for seats not from opposing sides but from within the same party. As a result, the inevitably victorious PDCI-RDA was fully in control of the Territorial Assembly and, in line with the provisions of the *loi-cadre,* could form the colony's Government Council by appointing all ministers. In the meantime, Houphouët-Boigny continued his own ministerial career in Paris. Following the downfall of Mollet's government in spring 1957, he served in three more cabinets of the Fourth Republic, at one point—close to his past role as a doctor—as minister of public health and population. In light of the rapid succession of these governments and ministerial roles, he had hardly achieved any substantial results in his various duties when the escalating Algerian War and the resulting final crisis of the French Fourth Republic brought de Gaulle back to power in spring 1958.

The general asked Houphouët-Boigny to remain in Paris and join his government, and to help draft the constitution for the fifth iteration of the French Republic, specifically in relation to the overseas territories. This provided the Ivorian leader with a unique opportunity to leave his imprint on the French Community and to once more have the better of his Senegalese rival. Instead of including a federation of African overseas territories within, as advocated for by Senghor, the Community was to have a federal structure linking Paris directly to France's individual overseas possessions. This was ultimately the preferred solution of de Gaulle, who wanted to retain a stronger, more direct control. Although the Community, presided over by the general, was to elevate the French overseas territories to member states, they were not to become independent. While gaining autonomy, they would continue to rely on France for their foreign, defense, economic, and financial policies.

For Houphouët-Boigny, this was the ideal framework for the economic and social development of Côte d'Ivoire. He thus strongly promoted the Community during the campaign for the referendum on the new constitution, which confronted the African territories with the choice between membership and self-determination. To his great delight, the referendum of late September 1958 was a resounding success, not only in Côte d'Ivoire but throughout French Africa.

Yet the joy was tarnished by Guinea's rejection of the constitution, especially since it was an RDA-dominated territory. Houphouët-Boigny's frustration with the Guineans was probably only matched by de Gaulle's ire, who vindictively decided to make an example of them. Punishing Guinea for breaking with France, Paris abruptly withdrew all aid and personnel, and in the process the French took everything with them that was not nailed down. Moreover, the Élysée lobbied the White House not to come to the rescue of Touré and his fledgling country. The Ivorian leader supported these retaliatory measures, for not only did he take the no-vote as a personal affront, but the success of an independent Guinea could have discredited his own advocacy for the French Community. He was henceforth at odds with the Guinean leader. Isolated, stripped of support, and unable to find succor in the West, Touré turned to the East, seeking help from the Soviets and joining forces with Nkrumah.

The Ghana-Guinea Union became a focal point for the Ivorian leader, who not only mocked the two countries' military buildup as a costly distraction from development, but also saw the French-led Community defense as the most effective way to protect himself from their supposed machinations against him. Houphouët-Boigny argued that, unlike his Ghanaian and Guinean counterparts, he prioritized the economic and social development of his country, of which he became the prime minister following the legislative elections of April 1959 (see figure 2.1). Fully in charge of an increasingly all-powerful party and with a constitution granting him strong executive powers, he ruled Côte d'Ivoire without challenge, and any criticism was largely confined to young RDA members and students.

In the region, by contrast, he was increasingly criticized for his continued and vociferous support of France's imperial rearguard actions. He was also concerned about the federative efforts of Senegal, which had formed the Mali Federation with French Sudan

FIGURE 2.1. Government of Côte d'Ivoire, 1959. *Front row, left to right:* Auguste Denise (minister of state), Félix Houphouët-Boigny (prime minister), Philippe Yacé (president of the Territorial Assembly), Jean-Baptiste Mockey (deputy prime minister, in charge of the Ministry of the Interior), and Jean Delafosse (minister of state); *second row:* Amadou Koné (public health), Ernest Boka (civil service), Georges Monnet (agriculture and cooperation), Raphaël Saller (finance and planning), Alphonse Boni (justice), Konan Kanga (secretary of state for finance), and Koffi Ahoussou (secretary of state for industry and planning); *third row* (secretaries of state): Charles Donwahi (agriculture), Jean Konan Banny (youth and sport), Jean Thès (post and telecommunications), Amadou Bocoum (information), Camille Gris (labor and social affairs), Jean Millier (public works), and Alcide Kacou (technical education). Courtesy of Fondation Félix Houphouët-Boigny.

in April. Simultaneously fearful of the further expansion of this federation and the regional influence of the future state of Nigeria, in May he established—together with Dahomey, Upper Volta, and Niger—the Council of the Entente, which he would informally lead and hold together by providing financial support. Instead of shifting his position on the relationship with the colonial power, and despite complaining about his regional predicament to French high commissioner in Côte d'Ivoire Yves Guéna, he remained undeterred.

Moreover, as in the case of the *loi-cadre,* he promoted the Community in the United States, this time directly with President Dwight D. Eisenhower and his assistant secretary of state for African affairs Joseph C. Satterthwaite during a meeting in Washington in November. While also fishing for American aid and investment, he not only repeated his mantra that French protection benefited African development, but also portrayed the Community and himself as bulwarks against communism in Africa. Having invested so much political capital into the Community both publicly and behind the scenes, Houphouët-Boigny thus received a major blow when it came crashing down by the end of the year.

Defying the General

Despite increasing regional headwinds against the Community, the Ivorian leader was resolute. During the Community's executive council meeting of mid-December 1959, he reiterated his faith in the Franco-African construct as the best protection against the expansionist Pan-African ambitions of Nkrumah and Touré. The irony was that immediately after the meeting, de Gaulle gave in to growing African nationalist and international pressures and publicly recognized the Mali Federation's desire for independence. This meant the end of the Community, which, together with Houphouët-Boigny's reputation, lay in tatters.

But rather than admitting defeat, the Ivorian prime minister rose once more to the challenge and, in order to restore his political clout and prospects, took the fight to the French president. In anger, he also temporarily lost much of his respect and admiration for de Gaulle, and mockingly observed to the American consul in Abidjan that the "General himself does not know what he wants or where he is going."[9] Houphouët-Boigny, by contrast, knew what he wanted, namely, to restore his African nationalist and leadership credentials by obtaining for Côte d'Ivoire and the other Entente states a better deal than Mali received from France, one with independence and a postcolonial relationship on his terms. This led, unlike in British West African colonies such as Nigeria, to an abrupt rather than a planned transfer of power.

Before going on the offensive, the Ivorian leader first wanted to see how the Franco-Malian negotiations would play out and, more importantly, to strengthen the cohesion of the Entente by aligning the policies and expectations of its leaders. Although the Ivorian authorities were preparing the ground for independence in spring 1960, the overly self-confident French did not see what was coming. They expected the Entente states to be part of a "renovated Community," and to delay their independence until 1961 to allow for the signing of cooperation agreements beforehand, as they were doing in Mali. But for Houphouët-Boigny, this was out of the question. Determined to outperform his peers in francophone Africa, he first wanted independence and would only then consider cooperation agreements. On 3 June 1960, he and the other Entente leaders—Hamani Diori of Niger, Hubert Maga of Dahomey, and Maurice Yaméogo of Upper Volta—thus formally asked for independence. Although the French government initially refused this request, de Gaulle and his lieutenants eventually had to give in to a united and steadfast Entente front. But during the negotiations for the transfer of power, which began in early July, they wanted to make the formal protection of Houphouët-Boigny and his peers by French forces conditional on the Entente leaders' commitment to entering cooperation agreements immediately after independence. Even though the Ivorian leader believed in the need for French military protection and temporarily wavered, he eventually held firm. The transition agreements of 11 July thus provided for independence without any strings attached.

Houphouët-Boigny had achieved a first significant victory that set him apart from Mali. But Paris feared that Côte d'Ivoire, and with it the other Entente states, was slipping out of its control and that this could have ramifications for its position in other former African colonies. The Ivorian leader actively played with and heightened these fears by cozying up to the United States and calling for its assistance by presenting himself as a guarantee against communist expansion in the region. Although the Americans were not yet willing to consider challenging Paris in its sphere of influence, the French high commissioner in Abidjan raised the alarm bells in the Élysée that Côte d'Ivoire seemed to have left the Franco-African Community for good. Simultaneously, however, Guéna also observed that the Ivorian government was still looking to France for protection and military assistance. This was the trump card that de Gaulle was determined to use to bring the Entente states into cooperation agreements, and thereby avoid an "anomaly" that could lead other former colonies to question and potentially renege on their agreements with France. The general thus let it be known in the Entente capitals that after independence, French forces would not automatically intervene to maintain public order, and that his government would only consider formal requests to do so on a case-by-case basis.

This tactic had the desired impact. Fearful of regional rivals and subversion, the Entente leaders, especially Houphouët-Boigny, continued to count on France's

FIGURE 2.2. At the proclamation of independence, 1960. *In front:* Louis Jacquinot (minister for overseas France) and Félix Houphouët-Boigny; *behind him, wearing black glasses:* Jean Delafosse (president of the Economic and Social Council). Courtesy of Fondation Félix Houphouët-Boigny.

security umbrella and assistance after celebrating their countries' independence in early August 1960 (see figure 2.2). President of Côte d'Ivoire since then, he thus approached de Gaulle in September to start the negotiations for cooperation agreements that, in addition to defense and military assistance, were to cover pretty much everything from economics and finances to education and culture. The main test of strength with de Gaulle was yet to come, however, and would center on the future postcolonial security relationship between France and the Entente, which Houphouët-Boigny sought to establish outside of the "renovated Community." This infuriated the general, who wanted to retain the Entente within the French sphere of influence in Africa, aimed for a common defense organization therein, and expected a clear commitment in return for military assistance, not least to avoid alienating such countries as Senegal, which had parted ways with Mali. But the Ivorian leader was in no mood to give in, and in October he clearly voiced his ongoing frustration, if not anger, with France to the French high commissioner in Abidjan: "I no longer want to ask anything of France. . . . For two years, I have received nothing of what I asked for; I have been mocked, my dignity has been trampled upon, and I will no longer accept these bargains."[10]

Yet the rant was probably part and parcel of Houphouët-Boigny's negotiation strategy, for not only did he still want something from France, but he was also ready to haggle. During a meeting with the other Entente leaders in Ouagadougou in early January 1961, he raised the specter of Ghanaian and Soviet expansionism and subversion and argued that the Entente states needed not only their own national armies and defense coordination but also a defense alliance with and military assistance from France. This assessment and position were accepted by his peers, but the question was the format and framework the Franco-Entente military alliance would have, and whether it would be acceptable for the Élysée.

During meetings in Paris in mid-January, first Prime Minister Michel Debré and then de Gaulle made it clear to Houphouët-Boigny that if the Entente sought, unlike France's other former African colonies, a defense relationship apart from the "renovated Community," it would not be entitled to the same level of support. But the Ivorian president was not intimidated by these threats, and the Entente put forward draft cooperation agreements that were strictly bilateral and without any reference to the Community. This infuriated policymakers in Paris, and Debré tried once more to make it clear to Houphouët-Boigny that a common defense was a prerequisite for a French commitment. In response, the Entente leader showed a willingness to compromise by raising the possibility of a multilateral agreement with the Entente rather than just bilateral ones between its members and France. Simultaneously, however, he also resorted to the hardly veiled threat that the Entente states could turn to other countries for support. In combination with reassurances from Houphouët-Boigny that he was not motivated by anti-French sentiments, this threat led to a realization in Paris that inflexibility would only play into the hands of radical African states and the Soviet bloc, while potentially leading to increased American influence in the region. As a result, French policymakers grudgingly opted for a middle course that would bring the Entente states into a common framework yet separate from the "renovated Community."

Though largely symbolic, this was the political victory that the Ivorian president had hoped for and that he seemed able to sell to his fellow Entente leaders. Though while he publicly displayed his satisfaction, he nevertheless kept up the pressure on the French during the negotiations for the cooperation agreements by continuing to flirt with the Americans. The resulting French willingness to continue to compromise came in handy when in February 1961 Upper Volta's Yaméogo suddenly refused to play along. In a challenge to Houphouët-Boigny motivated by jealousy, he refused to be part of the multilateral defense agreement and to host French military bases on his country's soil. Although de Gaulle categorically reiterated to the Entente leaders in a meeting in March that there had to be solidarity in defense, the French were eventually willing to give in. While the multilateral defense agreement would be between France, Côte d'Ivoire, Dahomey, and Niger, the military assistance agreements would be bilateral and with all Entente member states, including Upper Volta. The Ivorian leader had managed to wrest this final compromise from Paris by insisting that by cutting Yaméogo off, he would be driven into the arms of a radicalizing Mali.

In the end, Houphouët-Boigny managed to secure continued French protection, hold the Entente together, and obtain a tailor-made postcolonial relationship for Côte d'Ivoire and the other Entente states by showing his African peers that he was standing up to France. With the Ivorian president visibly satisfied, the cooperation agreements were signed on 24 April 1961. Following his dramatic transformation from imperial nemesis to cheerleader, Houphouët-Boigny had thus not only succeeded in salvaging his political career from the ruins of the French empire, but also in establishing the postcolonial relationship with France on his terms. While continuing to depend on France's protection and assistance, he had gained a substantial degree of room for maneuver. This simultaneous dependence and independence would provide the parameters for his upcoming "Cold War."

3

"Cold" Warrior

> Now, Côte d'Ivoire is very anti-communist. Indeed, Ivorian nationalism exists, and this is fortunate because the Ivorian is a farmer. He lives off his land and lives very well thanks to it. Therefore, he is attached to his land, and thus to his country. He is ready to defend his property against communism. Côte d'Ivoire is a rich country; it simply needs to become aware of this situation, and the Ivorian, quite naturally, will be anti-communist.
>
> —Félix Houphouët-Boigny, 26 September 1961

By the time Houphouët-Boigny made this anti-communist profession to the Ivorian Defense Committee, the Cold War had definitely arrived in Africa. In the wake of the "Year of Africa," when seventeen colonies achieved independence in 1960 (see map 3.1), and after Soviet advances into West Africa, notably in Guinea and Ghana, the superpowers and their allies competed for influence in the region. This process had been substantially accelerated by the outbreak of the Congo crisis in 1960 and the murder of Congolese prime minister Patrice Lumumba by Moïse Tshombe's Katanga in collusion with Western

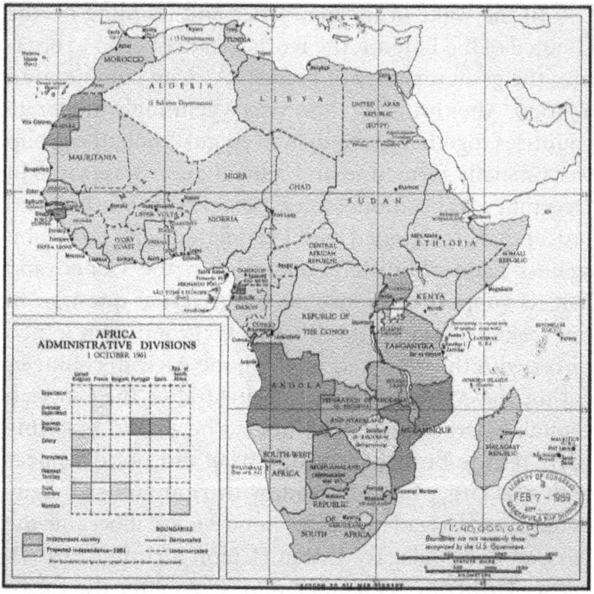

MAP 3.1. Africa, 1961. Library of Congress, Geography and Map Division.

and neocolonial forces in early 1961. This in turn contributed to the division of the newly independent African countries into the radical Casablanca bloc and the moderate Monrovia group. While this *external* Cold War characterization of the two groupings was influenced by their respective Eastern and Western orientations, their main differences were more *internal* and revolved around their competing visions for the African continent, regional integration and cooperation, economic and social development, nonalignment, and relations with the former metropole. Houphouët-Boigny played a central role in this inter-African bloc building and resulting competition.

In the wake of independence and building on the Council of the Entente, the Ivorian leader began to organize the great majority of France's African colonies into a group. After bringing these overwhelmingly moderate countries together in Abidjan in August 1960, the group was officially formed in and named after Brazzaville in December. Its positions seemed clearly pro-Western and pro-French, for it sided with President Joseph Kasavubu against Prime Minister Lumumba in the Congo and lent its support to France on the Algerian question in the United Nations. The Brazzaville group then joined forces with the moderate anglophone African countries within the Monrovia group, named after the Liberian capital, where its first meeting had been held in spring 1961. Yet the Brazzaville group itself did not disappear with this larger bloc. Instead, with Houphouët-Boigny determined to lead in francophone Africa, it became the African and Malagasy Union (Union africaine et malgache, UAM) in September 1961. Even after the establishment of the Organization of African Unity (OAU) in May 1963, rather than dissolving, the UAM was transformed into the African and Malagasy Union for Economic Cooperation (Union africaine et malgache de coopération économique, UAMCE) in March 1964, which was then itself reinvented as the African and Malagasy Common Organization (Organisation commune africaine et malgache, OCAM) in February 1965.

Nevertheless, in its earlier iterations, the francophone Brazzaville group cooperated extensively with the anglophone Monrovia powers, notably Nigeria. The Ivorian president shared with Nigerian prime minister Abubakar Tafawa Balewa a pro-Western outlook, an affinity for the former colonial power, anti-communism, a preference for cooperation instead of integration in

Africa, and, probably most importantly, a strong enmity towards Nkrumah. The Ghanaian president was a key protagonist of the opposing Casablanca bloc, which was also named after the city where the group had first assembled in January 1961. This smaller bloc's vision for a more integrated Africa lost out against that of the Monrovia group in the establishment of the OAU, which was a far cry from Nkrumah's Pan-Africanist ideals. Moreover, the increasingly radical and authoritarian Ghanaian leader became more and more isolated in African affairs prior to his overthrow in early 1966. While there are only rumors about Ivorian and French involvement in this coup, Abidjan had clearly been working against Accra.

In confronting Nkrumah and fighting his "Cold War" more generally, Houphouët-Boigny worked closely with Paris. In the decade and a half from the end of the Second World War to independence, the Ivorian leader had transformed not only from an ally of the French communists to a staunch anti-communist, but also from imperial nemesis to, first, imperial cheerleader and then key ally in France's neocolonial endeavor in Africa. Following the clash with de Gaulle during the transfer of power, the tailored Franco-Entente cooperation agreements put the relationship between Abidjan and Paris on a firm footing. Already during the negotiations for these agreements but especially thereafter, the Ivorian president worked and conspired closely with the general's "Monsieur l'Afrique," Jacques Foccart (see figure 3.1). Heading the General Secretariat to the Presidency of the Republic for the Community and African and Malagasy Affairs, Foccart was in charge of France's African policy and served as the intermediary between de Gaulle and francophone African leaders, among whom

FIGURE 3.1. With Charles de Gaulle and Jacques Foccart at the Élysée, 1961. Courtesy of Fondation Félix Houphouët-Boigny.

Houphouët-Boigny became the most important. Yet inasmuch as he had never been a communist, despite his political affiliation with the PCF, his neocolonial collusion with the former colonial power did not mean that he was just taking orders from Paris.

As this chapter will show, the Ivorian president skillfully relied on Paris in waging his very own regional Cold War. While he obligingly served France in pursuit of its neo-imperial agenda in the region, he leveraged French power and resources to protect himself and his regime at home, to extend and strengthen his influence in francophone Africa and West Africa, and to build a continental bulwark against radical forces on the continent. While increasingly buying—unlike France—into the narrative of a communist onslaught in Africa, he also adroitly employed Cold War logic to garner support and allies. In essence, however, he was driven by his ambition to strengthen Côte d'Ivoire and, by extension, his regime and security and to expand his leadership role and influence in the region. This agenda and its underlying motivations drove Houphouët-Boigny in his rivalry with Nkrumah, foray into Congolese politics, support for Biafra's secessionist struggle against his former ally Nigeria, and partnership with apartheid South Africa.

Archenemy

In September 1958, confident of French protection through the Community, Houphouët-Boigny mocked Nkrumah and the Ghanaian armed forces in a speech to the Ivorian people and political class at Abidjan's Géo André Stadium: "Do you believe . . . these billions that our great friend Kwame Nkrumah will invest in a military organization will serve any purpose other than false prestige? . . . Can Kwame Nkrumah truly attack any territory, even if he intended to?" His own answer to this clearly rhetorical question was "I do not think so."[1] But with independence, Cold War escalation in Africa, and mounting inter-African rivalry, his tune came to change dramatically. First concerned by Ghanaian subversion, the Ivorian leader then increasingly saw, or at least portrayed, Nkrumah as a communist spearhead in Africa and became even worried by Ghana's conventional military potential. In response, he wanted to rely on and strengthen French military support and protection, positioned himself and Côte d'Ivoire as anti-communist bulwarks in the region, called on Washington for assistance—even if mainly to extract additional support from Paris—and joined forces with like-minded West African powers, notably Nigeria, in confronting and scheming against Nkrumah. What had begun as a seemingly lighthearted development competition in 1957 turned the relationship between the two West African leaders, despite their shared Akan heritage, into one of the most hostile rivalries of early postcolonial Africa.

Beyond their competing visions for development, Houphouët-Boigny and Nkrumah also disagreed on the postcolonial future of Africa. While the former wanted to retain the colonial boundaries and remain in a federation or at least a close relationship with France, the latter aimed to fully decolonize and integrate the continent in line with his Pan-Africanism. Following the establishment of the Ghana-Guinea Union, which was joined by Mali in 1960, Côte d'Ivoire and the Entente rapidly became an obstacle to Nkrumah's more immediate regional ambitions for influence and integration. After initially trying to win over Abidjan diplomatically, Accra began to publicly lambaste Houphouët-Boigny's pro-Western positions and, especially, support to France's neo-imperial ambitions. Disagreement rapidly turned into dislike in Abidjan too. Already in November 1958, the Ivorian leader had warned Paris that he was exposed to Ghana's power and machinations. Thereafter, the specter of the Ghanaian threat came to serve a dual purpose in the Franco-Ivorian relationship. While for Abidjan it was a means to extract additional support from France, it allowed Paris to reinforce Côte d'Ivoire's reliance on French protection and military assistance. Paradoxically, rather than preventing Franco-Ivorian collusion, Nkrumah thus came to serve it.

The threat emanating from Ghana already seemed tangible in the run-up to independence, notably in relation to Accra's role in the Sanwi question. Based on a treaty from 1843 between France and the Sanwi Kingdom, Sanwi partisans in the Aboisso region wanted to gain independence by seceding from Côte d'Ivoire. With Nkrumah offering a safe haven and a platform to Sanwi refugees in Accra, Houphouët-Boigny inevitably saw him behind their agitations. From his perspective, which he shared with the French, Accra's support to the Sanwis was part of a broader expansionist plan to absorb Togo and Côte d'Ivoire's Aboisso region. This was pure speculation, however, for Nkrumah did not even go as far as to support calls from some quarters for the unification of the Sanwi territory with Ghana based on a common Nzema heritage. In fact, with Côte d'Ivoire's independence, Nkrumah tried to mend fences with a diplomatic initiative. But the resulting meeting with his Ivorian counterpart in the Ghanaian town of Half Assini on 19 September 1960 only reinforced Houphouët-Boigny's suspicions. Apparently, rather than offering reassurances, the Ghanaian leader insinuated that his country had a legitimate claim to the Sanwi region. Even worse, the Ivorian president returned from the meeting with the conviction that Nkrumah was after his life.

The Ivorian leader's takeaway from the meeting was most likely overly dramatic. But against the background of the Congo crisis and the emerging hostility between radicals and moderates in Africa, the Ghanaian leader even reinforced his support to Ivorian opposition groups, notably to the Sanwi. In an apparent show of support to Houphouët-Boigny, in January 1961 the French warned him about Nkrumah's machinations and emphasized that they refused to engage with the appeals addressed to them by the Sanwi. This show of solidarity while simultaneously pointing at the Ghanaian leader was part and parcel of France's strategy to get Côte d'Ivoire and the Entente into defense and military assistance agreements.

Yet Abidjan did not really need any convincing when it came to Nkrumah. His accelerated strengthening of the Ghanaian armed forces with Soviet bloc assistance in the wake of the Congo crisis made the Ivorian regime fear Ghana not only as a source of subversion but also as a conventional external threat. This fear was clearly on display during the Ivorian Defense Committee's meeting of September 1961. Defense Minister Jean Konan Banny first raised the Ghanaian armed forces as a threat to Côte d'Ivoire. Houphouët-Boigny then doubled down on his belief that Nkrumah wanted to align all African countries, if necessary by force, under his Pan-Africanist leadership. This, he implied, was part of a communist onslaught on Africa. In order to counter this threat, he argued, Côte d'Ivoire required a French military presence on its soil. By early 1962, fears of Ghana's increasing military might and expansionist agenda had begun to supersede the threat of subversion, and Houphouët-Boigny thus called on France for more military assistance and increasingly raised the possibility of complementary aid from the United States.

The Ivorian president was aware that raising the prospect of leaning on Washington provoked fears in Paris of being substituted by the Americans in France's sphere of influence, and made the French more willing to give him what he wanted. Meanwhile, however, he was also frustrated by American president John F. Kennedy's charm offensive in Africa, which aimed to win back such radical leaders as Nkrumah. From Houphouët-Boigny's perspective, the Ghanaian leader was the villain who stood in the service of Moscow, while he was the anti-communist bulwark that prevented Africa from being overrun by the Soviets. Washington should thus not woo Nkrumah and spend on Ghana but listen to him and provide assistance to Côte d'Ivoire. Although the Kennedy administration saw him as part of the old guard and had doubts about his long-term political survival, it nevertheless considered his insights on African affairs useful and was willing to give limited development aid to his country. He was also

FIGURE 3.2. With the Kennedys at the White House, 1962. President John F. Kennedy and First Lady Jacqueline Kennedy stand in front of the Grand Staircase prior to a dinner in honor of Félix and Marie-Thérèse Houphouët-Boigny. Behind them are (*left to right*) Henri Konan Bédié, Côte d'Ivoire ambassador to the US; R. Borden Reams, US ambassador to Côte d'Ivoire; General Chester V. Clifton, military aide to President Kennedy; Brigadier General Godfrey T. McHugh, air force aide to President Kennedy; Virginia Rusk; Dean Rusk (mostly hidden), US secretary of state; and Captain Tazewell Shepard, naval aide to President Kennedy. Photograph by Robert Knudsen. Courtesy of the John F. Kennedy Presidential Library and Museum, Boston.

not completely neglected in Kennedy's charm offensive and was invited for a glamorous state visit to Washington in May 1962, which temporarily gave him the public recognition he had been craving—even though the star of the visit apparently was, at least in the American president's eyes, his wife Marie-Thérèse (see figure 3.2). But despite being frequently irritated with Nkrumah, the Kennedy administration did not see him as a military threat to his neighbors. The Americans were thus reluctant to provide military assistance to Côte d'Ivoire, especially because the French, of whose sensitivities they were perfectly aware, seemed to have the situation under control. Nevertheless, the flirt with Washington allowed Houphouët-Boigny to extract the additional military assistance he believed he needed to strengthen the Ivorian armed forces against the Ghanaian threat, which in turn permitted the French to secure and even strengthen their security role in Côte d'Ivoire.

In early 1963, it seemed as if the Ivorian president's fears had become reality and Nkrumah had moved into action. On 13 January, President Sylvanus Olympio of Togo was assassinated in a coup. Although there was no tangible proof of Ghanaian involvement, only the circumstantial evidence of the historical enmity between Nkrumah and Olympio and Ghana's velleities for Togolese territory, numerous African leaders held Accra responsible. This was especially the case of Houphouët-Boigny, whose hostile position towards Nkrumah was shared by Balewa's moderate Nigeria, which also saw itself as threatened by Ghanaian subversion. After having grown closer in an increasingly divided postcolonial Africa, the West African heavyweights Côte d'Ivoire and Nigeria led the Monrovia bloc's diplomatic response to Olympio's assassination. In blaming Nkrumah, they aimed to ostracize him and remove his influence in the emerging OAU. However, their reaction to the Togolese coup and the Ghanaian leader's supposed involvement therein went beyond mere diplomacy. In March 1963, Abidjan and Lagos were entertaining the idea of intervening militarily in Togo with the dual aim of discouraging military coups and dictatorships in the region and assisting Togolese leader Nicolas Grunitzky, who had not been among the putschists, in establishing a stable government. But the plan was nipped in the bud by de Gaulle, who, because any Ivorian military adventurism was unthinkable without French support, had been consulted by Houphouët-Boigny. The general vetoed the plan because he feared an escalation that could transform Togo into a Cold War battleground and, probably most importantly, wanted to keep Nigeria out of francophone West Africa.

Any more forceful measures aimed at Ghana seemed unnecessary anyway because Nkrumah was increasingly maneuvering himself into a corner. After failing to leave his imprint on the OAU, and even to secure a place on its Liberation Committee, he increased and radicalized Ghana's own support to the liberation struggle. While the moderates shared the ultimate goal of African liberation, they were irritated that in addition to hosting liberation movements, he also hosted opposition groups of independent African countries, and that in training guerrilla forces, he increasingly relied on the People's Republic of China. By the mid-1960s, the Ghanaian leader was thus ever more isolated on the African stage. In combination with mounting domestic tensions, this led him to resort again to diplomatic means to restore his influence in African affairs and salvage the 1965 OAU summit that was supposed to be held in Accra.

Yet whereas Balewa—under pressure from within his country and government—was willing to accept Nkrumah's olive branch, Houphouët-Boigny rallied the francophone African countries against him and participation at the summit. Even after the Togo affair had blown over, Abidjan remained fixated on Accra. Especially once Houphouët-Boigny had mended fences with his former RDA companions Keïta and Touré, Nkrumah remained the only external threat in Côte d'Ivoire's neighborhood. Insisting on the danger emanating from Ghana, meanwhile, was also a useful means for the Ivorian leader to obtain additional military assistance from France and to retain the French military base in Port-Bouët, next to Abidjan, despite Paris's defense reforms and overall force reductions in Africa. Almost comically, however, it was the wave of coups that swept through the region in late 1965 and early 1966, and eventually also removed Nkrumah from office and as a threat for Abidjan, which convinced the French to retain their military foothold in Côte d'Ivoire.

In the rivalry that had started with a seemingly innocent wager in 1957, Houphouët-Boigny had thus come out on top, even before Nkrumah's forceful removal from the competition. Yet the Ivorian president's regional politics and maneuvers did not always meet with success, as his excursion into Congolese affairs—beyond France's usual sphere of influence—would soon reveal.

Prelude in the Congo

Houphouët-Boigny did not seem satisfied by having the better of his regional rival, but rather wanted to take advantage of Nkrumah's increasing isolation and the resulting enfeeblement of the revolutionary camp in Africa to extend his reach and that of France beyond the *pré carré*. The target was the still unstable yet strategically located, vast, and resource-rich former Belgian Congo, which the Ivorian leader sought to bring into his francophone Africa in the mid-1960s. This required first a leader at the helm of the Congo who would accept siding with Abidjan and Paris, and then the willingness of Houphouët-Boigny's peers to welcome the Congolese leader into their group. In light of the chosen candidate, it was astonishing that he and Jacques Foccart managed to pull off this feat, even though the success was short-lived. They threw their weight behind none other than the former Katangese leader Moïse Tshombe, who was widely despised in Africa and much of the world as the murderer of Lumumba in collusion with the former colonial and other Western powers. Seemingly against all odds, "France's man in Africa" and de Gaulle's "Monsieur l'Afrique" succeeded in helping the disgraced Katangese leader to the Congolese premiership and into the fourth iteration of the Brazzaville group, OCAM.

Houphouët-Boigny had been anything but a friend of Lumumba and his supporters. In the first and most known chapter of the Congo crisis, like other moderates he had not supported the rightfully elected first Congolese prime minister. Instead, after Lumumba's illegal removal and arrest in autumn 1960, he gave his diplomatic support to President Kasavubu in the United Nations and African forums. Yet this was, in line with his conservative agenda for Africa, supposedly in support of Congo's integrity.

Paris, by contrast, wanted to break up the Congolese behemoth and thus supported the Katangese secession through its intelligence channels and by facilitating the provision of mercenaries—led by such infamous figures as Bob Denard—to Tshombe's regime. This shady assistance did ultimately not prevent Katanga's reintegration into the Congo by the United Nations in 1963, but it allowed for the forging of close links between Tshombe and the French intelligence establishment in Africa, headquartered in Abidjan. In the wake of Ivorian independence, and enabled by the cooperation agreements and a secret special convention empowering France in domestic security (see chapter 4), Côte d'Ivoire's capital became home to the main station of the African branch (Secteur N) of the External Documentation and Counter-Espionage Service (Service de documentation extérieure et de contre-espionnage, SDECE)—France's foreign intelligence service. Headed by Raymond Bichelot, a French pioneer of covert operations, the SDECE's station in Abidjan rapidly became the nerve center of the Élysée's machinations in Africa. Moreover, in 1963, Foccart dispatched his most trusted man for secret operations, Jean Mauricheau-Beaupré, to Houphouët-Boigny's side. The covert apparatus was thus in place when, towards the mid-1960s, Abidjan and Paris decided to help bring back Tshombe from his exile in Francoist Spain.

With the downfall of Fulbert Youlou in the Republic of the Congo (Congo-Brazzaville) in summer 1963, Foccart and Houphouët-Boigny lost a key player in their respective and complementary plans for a *pax gallica* and an "African family" of francophone leaders on the continent. With Brazzaville's lurch towards the socialist and revolutionary camps, they began to set their sights on the other (Democratic) Republic of the Congo (Congo-Léopoldville), still francophone but a former Belgian, and not French, colony. Tshombe, with whom French agents had remained in contact following his failed secession, was seen as the most promising way into the

Congo. Although he was a hard sell because of his image as the personification of the neocolonial stooge, from the Élysée's perspective he was the ideal candidate. While fiercely anti-communist, he was not, unlike commander in chief of the Congolese National Army, Joseph-Désiré Mobutu, Washington's man. Consequently, he had the potential to serve French interests against not only the revolutionary camp, but also the Americans. By 1964, the situation for the seemingly unthinkable return of Tshombe had also become more favorable. The Congolese government of Cyrille Adoula was running out of steam and was increasingly challenged by the Simba rebellion of former Lumumbists. In these circumstances, the former Katangese leader could bring multiple sources of Western, notably French, support, mercenary troops, and still significant influence in mineral-rich Katanga.

While assuring Tshombe of French backing, Mauricheau-Beaupré orchestrated from Abidjan a campaign not only to make "Lumumba's murderer" palatable in Africa, but also to portray him as the solution for a united Congo free from foreign interference. In addition to an influence campaign in the media, this undertaking required the active involvement of Houphouët-Boigny. Relying on his RDA network and specifically on Upper Volta's Yaméogo, who had evolved from challenger to faithful servant, the Ivorian president lobbied the leaders of francophone Africa in favor of Tshombe. These efforts proved successful because even the socialist and Pan-Africanist Keïta of Mali, who could not be suspected to serve a neocolonial cause but wanted to bring his country back into the francophone African fold, came to advocate for the former Katangese leader as the solution for the Congo. In combination with Tshombe's lobbying of Congolese stakeholders, this francophone

African support contributed to Kasavubu asking him to return to the Congo and form a government in early summer 1964. Consequently, the former secessionist became prime minister for the whole country, and stage one of Foccart and Houphouët-Boigny's stratagem was successful. The Franco-African intelligence complex then supported Tshombe in strengthening his regime and fighting the insurgents.

Whereas in the first stage of Foccart and Houphouët-Boigny's Congo gambit the latter's role had been somewhat limited, he came to play a central role in the second, more visible stage. This involved publicly and internationally defending the legitimacy of Tshombe's appointment as Congolese prime minister and, more importantly, to formally integrate him and the Congo into the Ivorian president's "African family." In December 1964, as a member of the United Nations Security Council, Côte d'Ivoire defended Tshombe in New York. In response to the Soviet representative's remonstrations that the Congolese government was a "puppet regime," Ivorian representative Arsène Usher Assouan insisted on its legality and that it was formally representing the Congo in both the United Nations and the OAU.[2] Meanwhile, Houphouët-Boigny's Côte d'Ivoire also defended and promoted Tshombe in Africa, where Nkrumah, one of the main backers of the late Lumumba and thus a potential critic, was weakened. Nkrumah lacked the clout to mobilize against the incumbent Congolese prime minister and his supporters, and ultimately to sabotage the Ivorian president's grand scheme. In early 1965, while keeping up the pressure on the Ghanaian leader, Houphouët-Boigny thus began to prepare the ground for bringing Tshombe into the concert of francophone African states.

Despite specifically having supported Tshombe's leadership bid, the Ivorian president nevertheless called for "depersonalizing the problems" of the Congo, arguing that "whoever was in power" in Léopoldville should be accepted in accordance with the principle of sovereignty enshrined in the OAU charter.[3] Following extensive lobbying of fellow francophone African leaders, the Ivorian president brought them to Abidjan on 25 May 1965 for a meeting with the specific aim to get their agreement in principle for the Congo's admission to OCAM. Although Mauritania, the Central African Republic, the Republic of the Congo (Congo-Brazzaville), Rwanda, and Cameroon—roughly a third of the organization's membership—boycotted the meeting, the Ivorian leader pushed through his agenda and obtained the approval of those present. The following day, the Congo, and with it its controversial leader, was admitted into OCAM. Illustrating the collusion between Abidjan and Paris, a few days later Tshombe was anointed in an audience granted by de Gaulle at the Élysée. It thus seemed that stage two had been successful too, and the conflict-ridden former Belgian Congo, with all its resources, was now part of Foccart's *pax gallica* and Houphouët-Boigny's "African family." But before they could even start reaping the fruits of victory, the whole scheme imploded or, rather, was blown up.

In October 1965, Tshombe was dismissed by Kasavubu, and the last remaining doubts about the political situation in the Congo were removed when Mobutu definitively took over the country in a coup in November. Abidjan and especially Paris saw this as a retaliatory act by Washington, a viewpoint that was in line with their mounting yet unjustified paranoia of an anti-French American agenda in Africa. What was certain, however, was that their strategy for central Africa lay in tatters after having lost first Brazzaville and then Léopoldville. In addition, OCAM, which had been inaugurated only in early 1965, was fractured by the Congolese episode. Yet inasmuch as the Ivorian leader was not giving up on his regional leadership, he continued to support Tshombe in his renewed Spanish exile and harbored hopes for his return to power. He even went as far as to sponsor a failed mercenary mission to the Congo in late 1967. Running out of options, Houphouët-Boigny had to accept that Mobutu was there to stay. By that time, his main regional focus had also shifted to Nigeria, where he endorsed the secessionist cause of Biafra.

Biafran Crusade

Houphouët-Boigny's meddling in the Congo acted as a prelude to his crusade for Biafra in the Nigerian Civil War (1967–70). This time, however, he ventured even further beyond France's customary sphere of influence and was not merely an accomplice but the conductor. In pursuit of a different yet complementary agenda to that of France, the Ivorian leader became federal Nigeria's main foe. This contrasted sharply with the early 1960s, when he stood shoulder to shoulder with Balewa in confronting Nkrumah. The West Africa and Nigeria of the late 1960s were very different.

The wave of coups that kept the region on tenterhooks during the middle of the decade also reached Nigeria, where Balewa was assassinated in early 1966. Yet this military putsch, which was largely the result of escalating political and ethnically driven divisions, was not the end of Nigeria's travails. A countercoup half a year later kept the country on edge, and then pogroms against the Igbos in the Hausa-Fulani-dominated North contributed to the Igbo-dominated Eastern Region's determination to part ways with the rest of Nigeria. On 30 May 1967, the region's military governor, Chukwuemeka Odumegwu Ojukwu, made the secession official by proclaiming the Republic of Biafra in Enugu. After a "phony war" period marked by an ineffective Nigerian blockade of the Eastern Region, the actual war began on 6 July when the federal government of Yakubu Gowon decided to employ force to bring the Igbos back into the fold.

The conflict defied Cold War logic. While Britain and the Soviet Union backed the federals, the Biafran war effort was supported by Gabon, France, Portugal, Rhodesia, South Africa, Tanzania, Zambia, and Côte d'Ivoire. Houphouët-Boigny occupied a key position in this seemingly paradoxical constellation, and motivated by his regional aspirations and own Cold War logic, he set up and drove Biafra's Franco-African arms triangle and eventually even brought the southern African white supremacists into the scheme.

In the wake of Enugu's unilateral declaration of independence, the Ivorian president at first did not see the need to get involved. While he harbored sympathy for secession, he hoped war could be avoided and considered Nigeria within Britain's and the United States' orbit. Once blood was being spilled, however, he secretly began to cheer for Biafra. He shared this bias in favor of Enugu but especially against Lagos with de Gaulle, who considered the implosion of the vast, populous, resource-rich, and thus potentially hegemonic Nigeria an opportunity to extend France's sphere of influence and economic interests into anglophone West Africa. Yet unlike de Gaulle, who officially opted for neutrality,

Houphouët-Boigny wanted to help Biafra. With Lagos receiving military assistance from a reluctant London and an enthusiastic Moscow, he called on Paris to support Enugu's military effort. In autumn 1967, he first obtained the general's approval to divert leftover oil royalties to be paid by the French company Elf Aquitaine; instead of flowing to Lagos, they would go to Enugu to help the Biafrans buy arms through their military logistics hub in Portugal. Then, in no small part thanks to Foccart's support and ingenuity, de Gaulle approved sending German and Italian weapons that had been seized in the wake of the Second World War to Côte d'Ivoire to be passed on to Biafra. Although any such covert assistance to the secessionists was opposed by the French foreign ministry, the general chose to listen to his "Monsieur l'Afrique" and "man in Africa."

The provision of a few decades-old weapons by France and whatever the Biafrans could secretly scrape together on the commercial arms market were clearly insufficient to allow the secessionists to withstand the onslaught of the increasingly well-equipped federal forces. In early 1968, Houphouët-Boigny thus called again on de Gaulle for the provision of Ojukwu's forces with arms and ammunition. This time, the general was willing to go a step further and provide French weapons. He made it clear, however, that the weapons would be sent to Côte d'Ivoire and it would be Abidjan's and not Paris's decision to pass them on to Biafra. This pattern, with the French president providing weapons in response to an appeal by his Ivorian counterpart, was repeated during the remaining first half of the year. De Gaulle was hesitant, insistent on the utmost secrecy, and, unlike Houphouët-Boigny, not ready yet to diplomatically support the renegade republic. On 14 May, the Ivorian president officially

FIGURE 3.3. With Omar Bongo in Abidjan, 1970s. Courtesy of Fondation Félix Houphouët-Boigny.

recognized Biafra, part of a small wave of recognitions by Tanzania's Julius Nyerere, Gabon's Omar Bongo (see figure 3.3), and Zambia's Kenneth Kaunda, who in liaison with Houphouët-Boigny had decided to break ranks with the OAU's pro-Nigerian majority.

Publicly, the Ivorian president explained his diplomatic support to Biafra on humanitarian grounds. This was, according to the French ambassador to Côte d'Ivoire, part of the explanation. But Jacques Raphaël-Leygues also saw the Ivorian leader motivated by a historical hostility to federations; an animosity towards the British and their historical reliance on what he considered the backwards Northern Nigerians; a fear that Nigeria could, as a whole, tilt the regional Cold War balance; and a skepticism towards military regimes. Yet Houphouët-Boigny was also driven by more sinister, religiously tainted Cold War security concerns. On 24 July 1968, in a dramatic appeal to de Gaulle to help Ojukwu, in whom he saw the potential to be "one of the best heads of state of all of Africa," he wrote:

> This is certainly in the interest of Biafra, but it is also about the future of the whole of Africa, which a blind policy pursued by France's Anglo-Saxon allies risks throwing into an extremely dangerous situation, with the malign influence of the Arab revolutionaries of Algeria and Egypt [who supported federal Nigeria] and the establishment of their Russian and Chinese Communist allies in the heart of this continent where, until now, Christians, animists and Muslims have lived on excellent terms, in fraternal collaboration.[4]

The Ivorian leader was thus concerned by a communist onslaught, spearheaded by Muslim Arabs supporting a federal Nigeria dominated by the majority-Muslim North. These concerns were compounded by his fears that these Arabs might come after him because of his proximity to Israel, which had built up the Ivorian civic service. Consequently, in his own Cold War reading, he had skin in the game, and thus wanted Paris to provide more and sustained military assistance to Biafra.

By summer 1968, his escalating appeals to the Élysée came to produce more tangible results. First, on 31 July, the French government publicly came out in favor of Biafra. Without formal diplomatic recognition, Paris recognized the Biafrans' right to self-determination. While this boosted Ojukwu's morale and determination to carry on with the struggle, in August, de Gaulle agreed to more substantial weapons deliveries to Biafra. The general was pressured not only by the Ivorian president but increasingly also by the latter's proxy in central Africa. Supported by the French ambassador in Libreville, Maurice Delauney, Bongo called on de Gaulle to send more weapons and even to provide military assistance personnel. This had led, by autumn 1968, to a functioning arms triangle between Abidjan, Libreville, and Paris, in which the Ivorian and Gabonese presidents received the Biafran requests, passed them on to the Élysée, and then were provided by Paris with the weapons to be delivered to Biafra, of course with France's logistical support. Although the arms deliveries mainly consisted, with the exception of some smaller artillery pieces, of small arms and light weapons, they nevertheless allowed Ojukwu's forces to carry on and at times even fight back. But exactly when the French arms and ammunition deliveries had become sufficiently substantial to make an impact on the battlefield, de Gaulle temporarily suspended them by calling their effectiveness into question.

Greatly troubled by the general's doubts, in late October 1968 Houphouët-Boigny dispatched his defense minister, Kouadio M'Bahia Blé, to Paris to plead for the resumption of arms deliveries. In addition, Houphouët-Boigny made again a dramatic written appeal to de Gaulle, in which he once more cursed the British, the Soviets, and their Arab helpers, and implored the French president to save Biafra and, by extension, Africa. The Ivorian president's case not only was supported within the Élysée by Foccart, but also compounded by pleas from Bongo and Ojukwu himself. This was sufficient to clear de Gaulle's doubts. Côte d'Ivoire's arms and ammunition stocks were replenished and weapon deliveries to Gabon resumed in order to allow Abidjan and Libreville to continue to equip the Biafran forces. Nevertheless, with the arms deliveries being dependent on the general's whims and insufficient to halt the shrinking of Biafra's territory, the Ivorian president, flanked by Bongo and aided by Nyerere, maintained the pressure on his French counterpart into 1969. This kept the arms triangle running relatively smoothly, only for it to be thrown into doubt with the general's departure from the Élysée in April.

By spring 1969, Biafra was steadily shrinking, and it was in no small part the French weapons that kept Ojukwu and his forces going. Since their provision had been dependent on de Gaulle's blessing, his resignation after losing the April 1969 constitutional referendum on decentralization and Senate reform—to which he had tied his political future—ushered in a period of uncertainty. While the Nigerians hoped they could convince the French government under a new president to abandon the practice, Houphouët-Boigny and his fellow travelers in Africa and the Élysée—Kaunda, Bongo, and Foccart—pleaded both directly and indirectly with President Georges Pompidou to continue to assist the Biafran military effort. By reiterating his anti-Islamic and anticommunist arguments and meeting with Pompidou in July, the Ivorian leader ultimately succeeded in salvaging the essential French element in the arms triangle. Simultaneously, however, he was also working to transform the triangle into a square, since he considered France's contribution insufficient and ultimately too fickle.

Back in February 1969, Houphouët-Boigny had already observed in a meeting with Bongo and Biafran representatives in Libreville that with not only Biafra's but also Africa's future at stake, it was necessary to make a pact with the devil, meaning South Africa and by extension Rhodesia. Focusing on Cold War, instead of racial, fault lines in Africa, and by taking Bongo with him, he thus sought rapprochement with Pretoria and Salisbury, particularly with South African defense minister P. W. Botha. By autumn 1969, this had led to a genuine security partnership and South Africa's integration into the pro-Biafran armaments scheme. In addition to sabotaging the potentially strong liberation voice that Nigeria represented and indirectly fighting the Soviet communists, the southern African white supremacists were motivated by the hope that Houphouët-Boigny and Bongo could put in a good word for them with the leaders of two key Frontline States—a coalition of southern African countries coordinating resistance to apartheid and white-minority rule—Kaunda and Nyerere, who also happened to support Biafra. Ultimately, however, their reinforcement of the Ivorian leader's military assistance scheme for Ojukwu's forces was insufficient to prevent the end of the secessionist republic. Despite Houphouët-Boigny's last-ditch attempt to salvage some leftover of the Biafran dream through diplomatic brokering, Ojukwu fled to Abidjan, and on 13 January his chief of the general staff, Philip Effiong, had to surrender.

The Ivorian leader's Biafran crusade, like its Congolese prelude, ended in defeat. Unlike in the Congo, however, he had been the architect and driving force of the covert support to Ojukwu. In contrast to the Élysée, he saw the Nigerian Civil War not only through a regional lens but as part of a fight against a communist onslaught spearheaded by Arab Muslims. It was this anti-communist reading that brought him into a secret security partnership with South Africa, from which originated his advocacy for diplomatic engagement with the apartheid regime in Pretoria.

A Bridge Too Far

On 30 October 1970, in a lengthy speech to party faithful at the fifth congress of his PDCI-RDA, Houphouët-Boigny made the case for peaceful engagement—"dialogue"—with

South Africa: "Our relations with countries where racial discrimination is rife undoubtedly contribute to the gradual achievement of racial equality. They discover in us other Negroes, other men, men like other men, and that is a good thing."[5] In presenting himself as an advocate for peace, African unity, and neutrality who was just as much as any other African afflicted by apartheid, he insisted that the solution to overcome it was not the use of force, but dialogue.

At a time when the African decolonization wave had broken against the obstinacy of Portuguese colonialism and Rhodesian and South African white supremacism, the OAU's Liberation Committee was supporting the freedom struggle, South Africa was increasingly isolated economically and on the international stage, and the Cold War was stoking the flames in southern Africa, calling for dialogue with South Africa was nothing short of controversial. The Ivorian president did so nevertheless, for not only was he convinced about the effectiveness of dialogue, but in recognizing South Africa's sheer economic and military might in the region and sharing its anti-communism, he also saw it as a useful ally in his African Cold War. What most of his critics did not know when he went public, however, was that he had been preparing the ground for his policy of dialogue over the previous years and had forged a secret alliance with Pretoria in the final stages of the Nigerian Civil War.

The Ivorian leader had already begun to test the waters in 1968, notably through his foreign minister, Arsène Usher Assouan, who tentatively raised the idea of dialogue with South Africa during a press conference early in the year. Although French diplomats were in favor of francophone African states engaging with

Pretoria to complement and help justify France's relations with and support to the apartheid regime, they did not want Houphouët-Boigny to go it alone and stir up further trouble in southern Africa. It seems that the Ivorian president was perfectly aware of the need for allies, and thus reached out to his predominantly francophone African network. His efforts encountered, however, only limited success. In addition to his comrade in arms from the Biafran crusade, Bongo, he only managed to rally Chad's François Tombalbaye, Madagascar's Philibert Tsiranana, and Niger's Hamani Diori to his side, who all saw South Africa as a means to diversify and strengthen their economy. On the margin of the OCAM conference in Kinshasa in early 1969, the five leaders agreed that Madagascar would spearhead the contacts with South Africa and the others would follow suit, and then Abidjan would establish diplomatic relations with Pretoria. This hypothetical plan, devised by a small and not necessarily determined group, was a meager result in light of Houphouët-Boigny's established leadership role in francophone Africa. Moreover, beyond his and France's usual sphere of influence, he managed to bring only the post-Nkrumah Ghana on board. This should not have come as a surprise, because not only could reaching out to apartheid South Africa be seen as a betrayal of the cause of African liberation, but the Ivorian president had also squandered political capital by going against the overwhelming majority of the OAU by supporting the Biafran secession.

Yet it was the very cause of Biafra that made, in Houphouët-Boigny's eyes, a rapprochement with South Africa necessary. During Tshombe's quest for leadership in the Congo a few years earlier, Côte d'Ivoire and South Africa had already been on the same side. While the Ivorian president was, as we have seen, a key political sponsor, the South Africans provided military assistance. But it seems that despite Mauricheau-Beaupré being the contact for both Abidjan and Pretoria, they had not come to rub shoulders. This required, as we have also seen, Houphouët-Boigny's Biafran crusade, despair over the reversals of Ojukwu's troops, and acute fear of a communist onslaught in Africa. In establishing this pro-Biafran security partnership, the Ivorian leader could rely on Mauricheau-Beaupré, whose contacts in Pretoria dated at least back to the Congolese episode and whose overtures were very much welcomed by P. W. Botha and the South African defense intelligence establishment. Simultaneous diplomatic approaches, however, were met with a certain degree of reluctance by the South African Ministry of Foreign Affairs, which perceived the communist threat primarily in southern Africa and first sought the Élysée's blessing. With this blessing forthcoming, not only the security relationship between Houphouët-Boigny and Botha but also the political one with South African foreign minister Hilgard Muller began to blossom during meetings in 1969. But South African hopes that Houphouët-Boigny, and by extension Bongo, would be able to help with the Frontline States were dashed. Tanzania and Zambia's partnership with Côte d'Ivoire and Gabon during the Nigerian Civil War was a marriage of necessity, and like the vast majority of African countries, they would not approve of Abidjan's proposal of unconditional dialogue with the apartheid regime. Consequently, when roughly ten months after Biafra's defeat the Ivorian president went public with his advocacy for relations with South Africa, he was met with outrage.

The policy of dialogue with South Africa that Houphouët-Boigny explicitly and publicly proposed for the first time at his party's congress on 30 October 1970 was anathema in a decolonizing and postcolonial Africa. Moreover, his assessment that the continent was confronted with a struggle between communism and anti-communism ran contrary to that of other key players, particularly the Frontline States. Zambia's Kaunda held up the Lusaka Manifesto, which had been adopted by the Fifth Summit Conference of East and Central African States in April 1969 and identified protracted racial segregation and colonialism as the root causes of conflict in southern Africa. Instead of a dialogue with Pretoria, this position advocated for the exclusion and isolation of South Africa on the African and world stages and the support of liberation movements in the region. This was ultimately also the line of the OAU, which backed the liberation struggle in southern Africa. Consequently, the Ivorian president's call for a dialogue with Pretoria was met with shock and anger by many of his peers in Africa, and it was therefore not surprising that his proposal for a conference to discuss engaging with South Africa a month after his shock announcement at the PDCI-RDA congress went unheeded.

Nevertheless, confident in the righteousness of his path and supported by Foccart, Houphouët-Boigny was not ready to give up in the face of what seemed like overwhelming political adversity. In late April 1971, he convened a press conference to lay out more extensively his rationale for a dialogue with South Africa. Reiterating that he, like the other African heads of state, felt revolted by and condemned the policy of apartheid, he insisted that diplomacy and not the use of force was the solution. Instead of fighting the South African regime, he argued, it could be brought to modify its racist views and ultimately abandon apartheid through engaging in a dialogue. This was the policy of which he wanted to convince his African peers. The results of his ensuing diplomatic efforts were, however, once more meager, and he managed to retain the support of only Madagascar, Gabon, and Ghana and to gain that of Lesotho, Malawi, and Liberia. These states did not have the necessary clout in African affairs to make a difference, and at the OAU summit in the Ugandan capital of Kampala in June 1971, his policy of dialogue was decisively rejected. He was even abandoned by Côte d'Ivoire's fellow Entente states, which chose to abstain in the vote. But rather than giving up, he chose to go it alone, and this eventually led him to invite South African prime minister John Vorster for a secret meeting in his fief of Yamoussoukro in autumn 1974. With Vorster's policy of détente in full swing, he apparently even succeeded in bringing Senegal's Senghor (see figure 3.4) and representatives of Gabon and Zambia to this meeting. Emboldened, Houphouët-Boigny then sent an Ivorian delegation for a visit to Pretoria in autumn 1975, a visit he probably planned during Vorster's secret meeting. By the middle of the decade, the climate had become more amenable to engaging with South Africa, and the OAU even chose to refrain from condemning individual initiatives of dialogue.

Despite this late, limited, and largely implicit acceptance of his policy of dialogue, Houphouët-Boigny had further discredited himself in the eyes of many African leaders and, irrespective of his claims to neutrality, had clearly shown on whose side he was in the African Cold War. Although his approach to South Africa largely complemented and assisted that of France, he did not simply serve the French cause in Africa, which had become less straightforward first following de Gaulle's

FIGURE 3.4. With Léopold Sédar Senghor, 1970s. Courtesy of Fondation Félix Houphouët-Boigny.

resignation in 1969 and then Foccart's departure from the levers of power in the Élysée in 1974. Always in pursuit of what he considered in the interest of his country, regime, and himself, the Ivorian president evolved—in a crescendo of foreign policy adventures—from accomplice to instigator and conductor. Regardless of setbacks, collateral suffering, and reputational damage, he carried on unrepentantly in his escalatory foreign policy trajectory. He thereby ended up backing the losing side in the Angolan Civil War against the Popular Movement for the Liberation of Angola (Movimento popular de libertação de Angola, MPLA), scheming against the revolutionary Burkinabe leader Thomas Sankara in the 1980s and supporting Charles Taylor in the Liberian Civil War towards the end of Houphouët-Boigny's life. These often-unsuccessful Machiavellian machinations, and especially those already deployed in the first one and a half decades of his reign, would probably have brought about the downfall of any other leader. Yet

Houphouët-Boigny not only could count on French backing, but also ruthlessly eliminated any potential opposition and secured the goodwill of many Ivorians by developing the economy and raising their living standards. A recipe that was ultimately too dependent on both him and external circumstances.

4

Enlightened Despot

> The happiness of the Ivorian people is our only goal, we have never stopped proclaiming.
>
> —Félix Houphouët-Boigny, 31 December 1959

Houphouët-Boigny boldly claimed that his only goal was the happiness of Ivorians while presenting the budget for 1960 to Côte d'Ivoire's Constituent Assembly on the eve of independence, shortly after his dream of the Community had been shattered. Although he now began to plan for a postcolonial future with independent economic and financial policies, his narrative remained unchanged—namely, that he wanted to develop Côte d'Ivoire to improve the lives of Ivorians. Houphouët-Boigny very much liked to style himself, in patriarchal fashion, as the father of the nation who only had the good of his fellow citizens in mind. Moreover, as in his publicly conducted diplomacy in Africa, he ostentatiously insisted on peace and dialogue at home. In front of the diplomatic corps in Abidjan in 1970, he stressed that "dialogue is the weapon of the strong, not the weak; it is the weapon of those who prioritize general issues over individual concerns and personal pride." He went on that "in the pursuit of peace—true peace, just and lasting peace—one must not hesitate for even a moment to resort to dialogue with persistence."[1]

As his rule and life progressed over the years, this insistence on peace and dialogue brought him the reverent appellations of *le sage* (the sage) and *le vieux* (the old man)—or the two combined as *le vieux sage* (the old sage)—in recognition of his wisdom and benevolence. Yet inasmuch as there was a secret, less peaceful side to his foreign policies in Africa, he could also be a scheming and ruthless leader domestically. Unlike his supporters and admirers, his victims and detractors came to see in him an old despot rather than an old sage. Both these characterizations fail to capture his rule, however, and in light of his mixed record and style of governance, "enlightened despot" would probably be more accurate.

In a rapidly changing decolonizing and postcolonial Africa, Houphouët-Boigny developed his own system of rule, the so-called *modèle houphouétiste.* Relying on and building upon his social, moral, and political authority, this model combined peaceful and coercive methods alongside rewards and punishments. After eliminating the political competition by integration and absorption, and the establishment of one-party rule, he co-opted what he considered key constituencies into his state. The rural elite, from which he came himself, was brought into and ultimately dominated the country's bourgeoisie. The different ethnic groups, meanwhile, were adroitly integrated into the state apparatus by applying informal quotas. The young and educated, who could have posed a formidable challenge to the aging "landed gentry," were given opportunities as technocrats in the governmental machinery. Small-scale farmers were made an integral part of the agricultural system, and numerous foreigners from such neighboring countries as Burkina

Faso gained employment and were welcomed by a government that advocated cultural and religious tolerance. A Baoulé chief and Catholic himself, the Ivorian president publicly advocated intercultural and interreligious harmony and dialogue.

Houphouët-Boigny's rule was very personal. In pursuit of peaceful resolutions, he frequently took it upon himself to mediate between conflict parties throughout the country and the economy, and to entertain the demands of different constituent groups ranging from public sector workers to students. Making an art of this paternal style of rule and offering a valve for frustrations within society, by the end of the first decade of independence he launched the *Journées nationales du dialogue* (National days of dialogue). Although the months of mass meetings with a whole range of constituencies representing the Ivorian society and economy were largely performative, they nevertheless made people feel heard and allowed the Ivorian leader to directly learn about and even address their grievances. Thereby, and in his rule more generally, he showed a certain magnanimity and largesse. This, however, was only possible because of the country's national wealth, which in turn relied on a well-functioning and growing economy.

In postcolonial Africa, hopes that independence would lead to a better life were widespread, and Côte d'Ivoire was no exception. Not only was Houphouët-Boigny perfectly aware of the hopes that the Ivorian people put in him, but he had also stimulated these hopes by insisting that economic development was his priority. This had been a key driver in his desire to stay under France's umbrella in the Community. Thereafter, and despite independence, he remained as confident as he had been when making the wager with Nkrumah back in 1957 that he had the right recipe to deliver. Once fully in charge of the country, he implemented a strategy of state capitalism that prioritized agriculture, infrastructure, and, to a lesser extent, industrialization and relied extensively on the influx of foreign capital. Thereby, he did not rely solely on France but, while never looking beyond the Iron Curtain, courted other Western powers, particularly the United States. To the dismay of the French, as in the realm of security, he did not hesitate to play them off against the Americans. Yet, when it came to economics, and as Abou B. Bamba has convincingly shown, it was not merely the specter of Washington's involvement: American capital and expertise in fact came to play a significant role in the development of Côte d'Ivoire.[2] This modernization strategy proved highly successful. Whereas regional competitors, despite employing similar methods to mobilize capital and aid—and, in Ghana's case, even playing the superpowers off against each other—failed to deliver, Côte d'Ivoire's economy took off with phenomenal growth rates. By the early 1970s, when the great economic disillusion had begun to take hold in many parts of independent Africa, Côte d'Ivoire thus stood out as an economic miracle from which not only the leadership but also ordinary people benefited. Before the Ivorians could reap the rewards of this success story, however, their president made certain through ruthless repression that they would not contravene his plans.

In the first half of the 1960s, when rivalries between African leaders and the Cold War kept West Africa on edge, a paranoid Houphouët-Boigny launched waves of repression in response to supposed plots against him. The first part of this chapter will deal with this increasingly authoritarian turn, which would be followed by

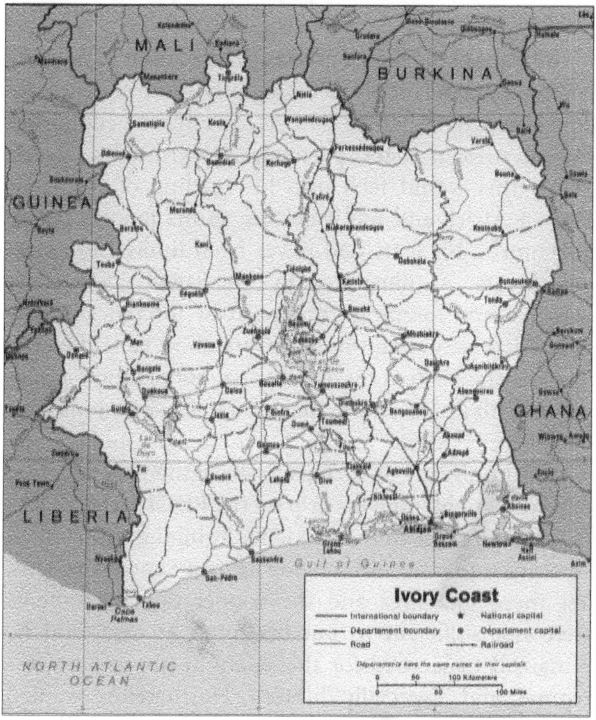

MAP 4.1. Côte d'Ivoire, 1988. Library of Congress, Geography and Map Division.

aftershocks and serve as a warning for the remainder of his rule. The second part then looks at the economic success story, which allowed the Ivorian president to reconquer the hearts of many Ivorians, after having struck fear in them. Yet the final part will show that the economy was built on shaky foundations, and that the *modèle houphouétiste* was dysfunctional and became, as a result of growing economic, social, and political pressures, ultimately unsustainable.

Sticks

In the wake of independence, and as discussed in the preceding chapter, Houphouët-Boigny became increasingly concerned by what he saw as communist-supported radical African states, particularly Nkrumah's Ghana. While this would feed into his reading of the Cold War in Africa and motivate him in his foreign policy adventures, his fears had never been limited to external threats. As illustrated by the Sanwi episode, he was first and foremost concerned by foreign, particularly Ghanaian-sponsored, subversion in Côte d'Ivoire. These fears whetted his appetite for cooperation agreements with France, particularly on defense and military assistance. Without waiting for these agreements to be signed, he already took steps to strengthen his fledgling regime by tightening his grip on the PDCI-RDA, cracking down on rebellious students, bringing disgruntled veterans into line, and moving against Sanwi partisans. Yet these measures and the cooperation agreements were not sufficient to put his mind at ease, and he remained concerned for the safety of his country, his regime, and, especially, himself. He therefore wanted the French to be militarily present in Côte d'Ivoire and to protect him from any real or perceived dangers from within. This would lead the Ivorian president to sign over his country's domestic security to France in early 1962, and then to count on French understanding and support in launching pre-emptive repressive waves when coups became a reality in his West African neighborhood in 1963.

Despite the signing of the cooperation agreements with Côte d'Ivoire in April 1961, French military planners were concerned that the Ivorian president could, in a further attempt to reinforce his image as an African nationalist, try to get rid of the remaining French military bases in his country. Yet even though the presence of the former colonizers' troops on Ivorian soil exposed him to criticism from such radical African leadership contenders as Keïta, Touré, and Nkrumah, Paris rapidly realized that Houphouët-Boigny had no intention whatsoever to get rid of them.

When he met with de Gaulle in early June 1961, he not only made amends with the general following their spat during the transfer of power but, due to the apparent threat emanating from his Soviet-sponsored radical neighbors, also asked for a strengthening of France's military footprint in Côte d'Ivoire. The Ivorian leader believed that he was exposed to the dual threat of African radicalism and communism, and that with French support and protection it was he who could hold it at bay in the region. During the following months he thus reiterated his request for a strengthened French military presence in Côte d'Ivoire, with troops moving into the bases in Bouaké and Port-Bouët as soon as possible. In light of defense reforms that entailed an increasing reliance on the nuclear deterrent and rapid-reaction forces, a strong military footprint in Côte d'Ivoire was far from a French strategic necessity. But Paris was willing to accede to Houphouët-Boigny's wishes, for he was indeed seen as a French asset and force multiplier in Africa. The Ivorian president, however, wanted still more from France than the staffing of its bases in Côte d'Ivoire.

Houphouët-Boigny wanted to make sure that even if he was threatened from within, the French forces would intervene and side with him. Whereas his young defense minister Konan Banny feared for Côte d'Ivoire's reputation in Africa and wanted to reduce the former colonial power's military footprint, the Ivorian president thus tried to secure a formal French commitment to his security. This led, following secret and alas undocumented negotiations with the French government and regional military command in early 1962, to a "Special Convention on the Conditions for the Potential Participation of the French Armed Forces in Maintaining Public Order on the Territory of the Republic of Côte d'Ivoire." Signed by Houphouët-Boigny on 9 February, this agreement consecrated the presence of French forces on Ivorian soil and stipulated that the Ivorian president could call on them for "logistical and communication support," and if faced with a "particularly serious situation," he could, "as an exceptional measure, request the intervention of the French armed forces."[3] In his quest for absolute protection, the Ivorian president signed over Côte d'Ivoire's domestic security to the French. This "Special Convention" was, however, of a secret nature. Had it become publicly known, it would have undoubtedly discredited Houphouët-Boigny's African leadership credentials and provoked vociferous condemnations from African nationalists, Pan-Africanists, and neutralists throughout the region.

But despite all the secrecy, the significant French military presence in Côte d'Ivoire could not be hidden. The Ivorian leader therefore felt compelled to justify it at least to his people and, in a speech to the Ivorian National Assembly in early 1962, explained the French military bases as an altruistic gesture by Paris that allowed Abidjan to focus on economic and social development instead of defense. The Ivorian people and members of parliament were blissfully unaware, however, that their president was pursuing more sinister motives, as would become clear a year later.

In 1963, francophone Africa was shaken by successive coups d'état: first in Togo, then in the Republic of the Congo (Congo-Brazzaville), and finally even in Dahomey, a close Entente ally of Côte d'Ivoire. These coups coincided with repressive waves in Côte d'Ivoire, launched by Houphouët-Boigny in response to supposed conspiracies to topple him and his regime. But in light of his preparatory measures for repression beforehand, it is more likely that the detonations of the coups in francophone Africa served as a fig leaf to reassert his control and make his regime bulletproof. Having obtained a French security guarantee and becoming increasingly paranoid, he embarked on a ruthless repressive campaign immediately after the coup in Togo.

When in the early hours of 13 January 1963 news reached the Ivorian president that his Togolese counterpart had been assassinated, he was at first shocked. This was not out of sympathy for Olympio, but rather out of fear that one day he could face the same destiny. Nevertheless, he had appreciated that the Togolese leader had stood up to Nkrumah, whom, as we already saw, Houphouët-Boigny held responsible for the putsch. Yet while externally he moved against Ghana, internally he struck within his own regime, seizing on the death of a fellow African leader as an opportunity. The blood in Lomé was not even dry yet when on 14 January, Houphouët-Boigny summoned the Ivorian political class to Yamoussoukro to announce a crackdown in response to an alleged communist plot against him. The next day he moved from words to deeds and dismissed Minister of National Education Joachim Bony, Minister of Agriculture and Cooperation Charles Donwahi, and Minister of Public Health and Population Amadou Koné from his government. The remaining half of the month saw the arrest of, among others, President of the Supreme Court Ernest Boka and at least fifty members of parliament, government officials, and members of the armed forces and gendarmerie. This far-reaching purge had been triggered, but not necessarily caused, by Olympio's assassination.

In hindsight, what hinted at Houphouët-Boigny's intentions was that he had already put the repressive apparatus in place beforehand. On 8 January 1963, his government announced the creation of a State Security Court aimed at dealing with subversive elements. Alarmed by Prime Minister Mamadou Dia's alleged coup attempt against Senghor in Senegal in December 1962, the Ivorian president wanted to be ready and have the tools in place when the opportunity to preemptively strike against any potential challengers presented itself. But the French, who were usually well-informed about security matters in Côte d'Ivoire, questioned whether there truly had been a communist conspiracy or internal plot against Houphouët-Boigny. The Ivorian leader thus launched a diplomatic offensive to convince the French and international observers more broadly that there had indeed been a plot against his regime. These efforts proved to be largely successful, at least with the French. On the ground, meanwhile, the purge was used to increase his security by replacing potentially critical voices with faithful ones, and to deter dissent by torturing prisoners and handing out harsh sentences, including the death penalty. Nevertheless, despite this purge and supposed plot, Houphouët-Boigny remained concerned by foreign subversion, especially from Ghana. These fears were further aggravated by his lack of trust in his own security forces. In pursuit of absolute security, he thus moved against his own army and gendarmerie. But for this he needed French help.

While residing in Paris in the summer of 1963, Houphouët-Boigny met with the French ambassador to Côte d'Ivoire to ask him for a meeting with de Gaulle to request French help to carry out a plan in response to yet another alleged conspiracy. This time, he argued, he was confronted with an even worse plot than the previous one, which involved some of his ministers and several MPs, sought to break up the Franco-Ivorian relationship, and was part of a Soviet-sponsored wave of assassinations in Africa. The Ivorian president thus wanted to request from his French counterpart "the support or at least the 'presence' of the French army during the few tense days he fear[ed] he [would] have to endure."[4] The plan was to temporarily disarm and purge the Ivorian army and gendarmerie with the protection and help of the French forces stationed in Côte d'Ivoire. Although there were concerns in Paris that such an involvement could compromise France, de Gaulle, advised by Foccart's general secretariat, agreed to give Houphouët-Boigny what he asked for in their meeting of 12 August. One day later, the Ivorian president launched, with French help, the disarmament campaign of the Ivorian security forces remotely from Paris. This coincided with the beginning of the uprising in the Congo, which by 15 August had led to the downfall of Youlou, whose regime had not been protected by the French. Paris feared the use of violence against African demonstrators, especially so shortly after having thrown off the reputational millstone of the Algerian War.

Following the coup in Brazzaville, concerns for France's reputation and the need to protect key allies in Africa came to play a role in the Élysée's decision-making. The French general in charge of Côte d'Ivoire and Ambassador Raphaël-Leygues were concerned that France, with its soldiers deployed in support of Houphouët-Boigny's disarmament campaign, could end up having to confront an uprising. They therefore called on the Ivorian president to return to Abidjan and rearm loyal army and gendarmerie units so that the French forces could step down. Their pleas remained unheard, however, and the Ivorian leader instead chose to remotely set up a militia composed of veterans and PDCI-RDA militants.

The issue was thus escalated to Paris, where the Council for African and Malagasy Affairs had to grapple with the question of how to provide a credible protection for France's allies in Africa without becoming embroiled in domestic troubles. Meeting on 22 August, the council—which was chaired by de Gaulle and attended by his Monsieur l'Afrique, ministers of foreign affairs, defense, and cooperation, and secretary of state for foreign affairs—came up with principles to inform any future intervention of French forces helping to maintain public order: France was not responsible for African armed forces, could but would not automatically intervene to maintain public order, and would strive to guarantee the security of heads of state upon request. In sum, Paris was willing to guarantee the personal security of its African allies, but not necessarily of their regimes.

When Houphouët-Boigny finally returned to Abidjan on 28 August, the French ambassador presented him not only with these principles, but also with the fait accompli that the support to his domestic disarmament campaign would end and the arms would be returned to the Ivorian security forces the very same day. Visibly taken aback, the Ivorian president grudgingly pretended to understand the decision. But realizing the limitations of French support, he chose to further strengthen his militia while trying to make amends with his purged army and gendarmerie. This did not mean that he had given up on his campaign to eliminate any remaining potential opposition to his regime with French help. When his close ally Hubert Maga was overthrown in Dahomey on 28 October, he tried to provoke the French into renewed support for his repressive endeavors by warning them that the coup in Cotonou was part of a major offensive led by communists and Egyptian president Gamal Abdel Nasser in francophone Africa, which risked being transformed into a Cold War battleground by the superpowers. The French did not take the bait, however, and Houphouët-Boigny thus embarked on yet another repressive wave. This time, he even forcefully cracked down on French citizens in Côte d'Ivoire.

Increasingly worried by Houphouët-Boigny's excesses, in November his ally and friend Foccart tried to rein him in, but not without first having to listen to his conspiracy theories. The Ivorian president insisted that he was confronted not with one, but three plots: an "African" one, led by his now former minister of agriculture Jean-Baptiste Mockey, that resorted to fetishism, witchcraft, and poison; a "Masonic" conspiracy, in which his now former defense minister Konan Banny played a key role, and that had communist connections; and an "international" plot, which was the brainchild of Ghana, Egypt, and French anti-Gaullists. Yet despite sympathy and friendship, Foccart did not buy any of these paranoid constructs. Instead, he told the Ivorian president to end the repression, punish those he considered guilty, and let the truly innocent ones off the hook. Without even the support of de Gaulle's man for African affairs, the by now despot had no other choice than to calm down.

This did not mean that the trials and tribulations were over for Houphouët-Boigny's suspects and victims. While not anymore that "spectacular," the arrests, torture, and condemnations continued into 1964, and did not even spare such close friends, political allies, and fellow planters as Ladji Sidibé. Illustrative of the methods of the purges, Sidibé, who had helped facilitate Houphouët-Boigny's political rise, was imprisoned on bogus charges, was tortured, saw his wife arrested and used against him, and was eventually sentenced to death. But like all others who received this ultimate sentence, he never had his death penalty carried out. Differentiating the Ivorian leader from other despots, the victims of the purges generally had their sentences quashed and were released a few years later, and in a good number of cases were reintegrated into the regime. A case in point was Konan Banny, who later recovered his position as defense minister.

The sheer arbitrariness and absurdity of the purges then came fully to the fore when the Ivorian president publicly admitted in the 1970s that the accusations of plots and conspiracies against him had been largely fabricated. Nevertheless, in addition to alleviating his increasingly paranoid threat assessment, the purges allowed him to streamline his regime and send a clear signal to any potential challenger. Finally, the abating of the waves of political repression did not mean that the Ivorian leader gave up on the use of force. This was notably illustrated by the so-called Guébié crisis in the late 1960s, in which the Ivorian army brutally repressed a Bété uprising in the Gagnoa region. But by that time, instead of repression, it was increasingly the Ivorian economic "miracle" that came to dominate the narrative of Houphouët-Boigny's reign.

Carrots

When Houphouët-Boigny ceremonially laid the first stone for the development of Abidjan's Riviera neighborhood in September 1970, he insisted that a "miracle, like a bet, is something that is prepared, conditioned, measured, decided upon, and realized through sheer willpower and perseverance."[5] By that time, Côte d'Ivoire was indeed witnessing what many observers described as nothing short of an economic miracle, which was epitomized by the dramatic growth and transformation of Abidjan into a major city that rendered the development of such new neighborhoods as the Riviera necessary.

Meanwhile, and although his regime pushed the miracle narrative itself, he was adamant that the economic success had not come out of the blue but was the result, indirectly praising himself, of hard labor and foresight. In a press conference in June 1974, he emphasized that "there is neither mirage nor miracle. It is the fruit of the efforts of an entire people united within our great Party, the PDCI-RDA, with the sole aim of freeing ourselves from the shackles of economic dependence." And two years later, during an official visit to France, he doubled down by stressing that "when it comes to the economy, a miracle is merely the consequence of good management."[6]

Despite later setbacks, Côte d'Ivoire's substantial economic growth in its first two decades of independent existence was indeed not a mirage, and its rising living standards were the envy of people in neighboring countries. Even though Nkrumah had long disappeared from the political scene by the 1970s, Houphouët-Boigny had clearly won their wager on the development of their countries. It is thus quite extraordinary that in 1970 the Ivorian leader compared his economic approach to a bet. While he certainly had a healthy dose of luck, he was no less convinced of his own righteousness and achievements. In looking at his economic policies, it is thus relevant to question their impact, and whether they lived up to his stated aim of throwing off "the shackles of economic dependence," particularly because of his close relationship with France.

Despite the implosion of the Community, Houphouët-Boigny continued—as in the realm of security—to count on France for the economic development of Côte d'Ivoire. The cooperation agreements thus also provided for special economic and financial relations between the two countries. This cooperation helped preserve France's significant position in the Ivorian economy, and was accompanied by extensive French advice, technical assistance, and investments. The Ivorian leader was nevertheless very much in charge, and independence allowed him to accentuate past approaches and capitalize on new opportunities. The Ivorian economy had, thanks to a postwar boom in agricultural production, substantially grown prior to independence. The Community's undermining of the federal structure, meanwhile, had already allowed Houphouët-Boigny to pursue more Ivorian-centered economic policies, and notably to retain more of the wealth production inside Côte d'Ivoire. The "unwanted" independence, however, gave the Ivorian president new levers with which to pursue his economic agenda, and even more autonomy in deciding with whom to share the spoils of wealth.

The starting point, for which the foundations had already been laid on the eve of independence, was the Investment Code. By offering favorable financial conditions, ranging from tax exemptions to protections for investments, it aimed to attract vast sums of capital to

Côte d'Ivoire to invest in the growth and diversification of the economy, as well as infrastructure. This implied that not only politically but also economically Côte d'Ivoire was firmly in the Western camp and managed to draw in substantial sums from France and the Western bloc more generally. Yet in contrast to the kind of liberalism prevalent in the West, Houphouët-Boigny opted for a much more dirigiste approach marked by state enterprises, government investment, and market intervention. The combination of this state capitalism with a large influx of money was, according to the Ivorian president, the right recipe to propel and diversify the Ivorian economy. This recipe was first and foremost applied to agriculture. This sector was obviously dear to a leader who was a major planter and had launched his political career as an advocate for Ivorian farmers. But it also provided a solid basis to build on, could easily expand on Côte d'Ivoire's vast uncultivated lands, and could diversify its range of crops.

The first of two key instruments in developing and diversifying agriculture was the Technical Assistance Company for Agricultural Modernization in Côte d'Ivoire (Société d'assistance technique pour la modernisation agricole de la Côte d'Ivoire, SATMACI). By drawing on international and bilateral aid, as well as channeling domestic and, especially, foreign capital, SATMACI focused on and invested in the training of farmers, the introduction of new agricultural techniques, the diversification of crops, and such farm inputs as seeds, fertilizers, and pesticides. To reduce the reliance on food imports, one crop received particular attention: rice. The government attributed such importance to this crop that in 1970 it even created a dedicated organization for it, the Company for the Development of Rice Growing (Société pour le développement de la riziculture, SODERIZ). Building on the efforts of the 1960s, by 1975 SODERIZ had achieved its aims to eliminate rice imports and satisfy domestic consumption, while even succeeding in exporting rice to neighboring countries.

This success and that of agriculture more generally were further enabled by a second key instrument, the Coffee and Cocoa Price Stabilization Fund (Caisse de stabilisation des prix du café et du cacao), which in 1962 resulted from the merger of two separate stabilization funds, one for coffee and one for cocoa, and was later extended to other agricultural products as the Agricultural Products Price Stabilization and Support Fund (Caisse de stabilisation et de soutien des prix des produits agricoles). This fund not only gave farmers security by guaranteeing minimal prices irrespective of price fluctuations on international markets, but also promoted exports and made investments in agricultural infrastructure. In combination with SATMACI, this led to the dramatic expansion and growth of the agricultural sector. Whereas the cultivation of ever more land and concomitant destruction of forests adversely affected the Ivorian ecosystem, Houphouët-Boigny's agricultural policies drove the country's economic miracle while benefiting both large- and small-scale planters.

Côte d'Ivoire's agricultural boom not only required foreign labor in large quantities, but also helped slow down urban migration by allowing family farms to survive and major plantations to thrive. The country nevertheless became increasingly urbanized. In addition to the growing governmental machinery and service sector, Houphouët-Boigny's industrialization efforts provided new job opportunities in cities. Although he prioritized the agricultural sector and diversification within it, he still wanted to diversify the economy as a whole. This required attracting investment and directing it to the industrial sector, which was largely in its infancy on the day of independence.

In the first instance, the Ivorian government's industrial policy was, in the aim of reducing reliance on imports, to provide substitute goods for imported products. Following the first decade of independence and faced with an already saturated domestic market, the policy was then adjusted to encourage the development of larger production units and the pursuit of foreign markets. These policies were complemented by efforts to attract multinational corporations to invest in and establish production units in Côte d'Ivoire. While the first industrial policy phase focused on agro-industrial products, the second one was aimed at manufacturing and material processing—for instance, in the textile and paper sectors. Meanwhile, Houphouët-Boigny's regime managed to attract, from a relatively early stage, such major corporations as Nestlé and Renault to invest and produce in the country.

The industrial sector was, admittedly, never in a position to rival the agricultural one. But its success should not be underestimated. Fired up by the government's financial and economic policies, it saw the creation of hundreds of companies and tens of thousands of jobs, and its share of GDP grew from 6 percent in 1960 to 20 percent in 1975 and came close to 24 percent in 1980.[7]

Although the industrial sector thus remained at roughly half the size of the agricultural one, it was nevertheless very much part of Côte d'Ivoire's postindependence economic success story. From independence to the late 1970s, the country experienced an average annual growth in GDP of well over 8 percent, with only one year of negative growth (1965) and such record years as 1964 and 1976 with 17.6 and 12.9 percent, respectively.[8] Moreover, this overall economic growth was not just absorbed by the country's rapidly growing population, which more than doubled during the same period from about 3.5 million to about 7.5 million.[9] GDP per capita experienced an annual average growth of almost 4 percent over the first two decades of independence.[10]

To put these numbers into perspective, Ghana had during the same period an average annual GDP growth just shy of 1.9 percent,[11] and a negative average GDP per capita growth of more than 1 percent.[12] The contrast between the two countries' economic performance could hardly have been more striking, and the divergence had already become apparent by the time when Nkrumah was overthrown in 1966. The political instability Ghana witnessed in its first decades of independence was certainly not conducive to economic development, but it would be negligent not to recognize the difference Houphouët-Boigny's policies made for Côte d'Ivoire's economic fortunes and, ultimately, those of his people. With a focus on economic and social development, he also provided, by whatever means necessary, a stable environment, as well as the infrastructure required for growth.

Transport infrastructure was obviously key in pursuit of the Ivorian president's economic vision. Agricultural produce, and to a lesser extent industrial outputs, had to be distributed within the country and exported abroad. The Ivorian government thus invested extensively in the development of a modern road network, including highways. While this helped connect the different parts and people of Côte d'Ivoire, its core aim was to efficiently deliver the agricultural goods to urban centers and, especially, ports for export. In combination with the dramatic agricultural expansion, this in turn required major investments in deep-water ports to handle ever-increasing volumes. While the existing port in Abidjan was substantially expanded, Houphouët-Boigny had another one constructed in San-Pédro. Meanwhile, and even though he was afraid of flying, the Ivorian president also invested heavily in air transport. Seeking both regional leadership and investors, upon independence he established Abidjan's international airport and transformed it into a regional hub by connecting it to major cities in Africa and the world. Moreover, he played a key role in the creation of the initially flourishing and now defunct multinational airline Air Afrique.

Combined with the country's dramatic economic growth, this national and international connectivity transformed Abidjan into a megalopolis that provoked admiration and envy, and attracted people from throughout the region and even the world. Centered on the business district of the Plateau, with its rising office buildings and skyscrapers, the city's appetite increasingly swallowed ever more land around Abidjan's lagoon and led to the establishment of such new districts as the Riviera, mentioned at the beginning of this section. But already from the early days of independence, Houphouët-Boigny wanted to give the city a certain splendor that would attract businessmen and tourists alike. This endeavor was almost immediately epitomized by the opening of the Hotel Ivoire in the emerging upper-class neighborhood of Cocody in September 1963. Thirteen stories high, and largely built by Israelis with Israeli money, the luxury hotel illustrated the Ivorian president's ambition to create an Ivorian equivalent of the French Riviera and by the same token build up a tourism industry in Côte d'Ivoire. Whereas the Hotel Ivoire did not fail to provide the background for glamorous evenings of the Ivorian high society joined by foreign dignitaries and luminaries, the broader ambition of an Ivorian Riviera did not materialize. This did not prevent Abidjan from developing into a major regional business hub that, like the Ivorian economy as a whole, became ever more energy hungry. The government of Houphouët-Boigny, by extensively relying on foreign, including substantial American, investment, thus embarked on successive building projects of hydroelectric dams. But despite ever bigger proportions, these dams struggled to keep up with the country's energy demands, not only from Abidjan, but from throughout the country.

While the lion's share of infrastructural investments was in Abidjan and other projects that Houphouët-Boigny considered economically essential or close to his heart, he also gave his attention and the country's growing wealth to other urban centers. After hosting Côte d'Ivoire's annual independence celebrations in Abidjan for the first few years, towards the mid-1960s he decided to rotate the festivities between the capital and provincial cities and towns—starting in 1964 with Bouaké—which he largely chose on political grounds. The choice was also influenced by real or perceived infrastructural needs, with major investments—for instance, in road and housing infrastructure—preceding and enabling the flamboyant celebrations. Meanwhile, the African doctor also showed that he cared about his people by heavily investing in medical infrastructure and care, again not only in Abidjan, but throughout the country.

Over time, however, "his" people could not help but notice that he was directing ever larger sums towards increasingly ambitious projects that, despite being presented as serving the common interest or a higher purpose, took on megalomaniac traits. Houphouët-Boigny had already favored investment in his hometown Yamoussoukro from his early days as a chief and leading planter. But after independence and especially during the latter stage of his reign, he transformed what not that long ago had been a village into Côte d'Ivoire's de jure capital. With the construction of a presidential palace and administrative buildings, Yamoussoukro formally succeeded Abidjan as capital in 1983. The crowning of this increasingly self-centered project was the construction of the Basilica of Our Lady of Peace in the latter half of the 1980s. Despite certain misgivings within the Vatican—not least over the basilica's disproportionate size and its dome dwarfing that of St. Peter's in Rome—Pope John Paul II personally traveled to Yamoussoukro on 10 September 1990, having already visited Côte d'Ivoire ten years earlier (see figure 4.1) to consecrate the basilica of the now ostentatiously devout Houphouët-Boigny.

FIGURE 4.1. With Pope John Paul II in Abidjan, 1980. Courtesy of Fondation Félix Houphouët-Boigny.

The Ivorian leader's ambitions for his country, meanwhile, were not only political and spiritual but also educational. Based on the French model of the *grandes écoles*—specialized, elite higher-education establishments—he established a range of institutions that focused on agronomy, public works, and engineering. As the specializations of these schools illustrate, Houphouët-Boigny wanted a return on investment, namely that the educational training directly served the Ivorian economy and society. Throughout Côte d'Ivoire, and especially in the country's business and academic center of Abidjan, he thus invested extensively in engineering and the hard sciences. This inevitably came at the expense of seemingly less beneficial and potentially critical humanities and social sciences. Nevertheless, tertiary, together with secondary, education received the lion's share of Côte d'Ivoire's colossal educational budget, whose 32.6 percent of governmental spending in 1973 was the biggest portion spent by any government on education in the world.[13] The Cinderella was primary education, which was purposefully neglected to keep people in the countryside.

Urbanization was, however, as unpreventable as the emergence of a critical Ivorian intelligentsia. When Côte d'Ivoire's economic fortunes dramatically reversed in the 1980s, and Houphouët-Boigny had fewer and fewer carrots to give away to compensate for his despotism, the educated urban classes became increasingly critical of his rule. Confronted with economic hardship, Ivorians woke up to the injustices in the country's economy and society, notably that their leader and his friends and family had been lining their pockets at their expense while much of the economy remained controlled, if not owned, by the former imperial power.

House of Cards

In 1983, writing from his exile in France, Laurent Gbagbo gave the Ivorian president and his party a devastating verdict: "The record of our country's management by one man, Houphouët-Boigny; by one party, the P.D.C.I. One word characterizes this record: dictatorship. The personal dictatorship of an individual supported by this single party of yes-men."[14] This teacher, historian, and unionist—who would go on to become the first and only politician to challenge the old sage for the Ivorian presidency—sought to refute Houphouët-Boigny's mantra that his one-party rule prevented ethnic division, guaranteed peace, and ensured prosperity in Côte d'Ivoire. Having experienced the regime's less peaceful and more repressive side as a political prisoner in the 1970s, Gbagbo argued that the country's earlier experience with multiparty politics before independence had not been organized along ethnic lines, that the records of other African countries such as Chad and Zaïre showed that one-party rule did not prevent civil war, and that most underdeveloped countries were governed by dictatorial regimes.[15] Following the end of one-party rule and Houphouët-Boigny's death, Côte d'Ivoire would in fact experience, if not ethnic, then at least identity-based politics, and ultimately descend into civil war.

But at the time Gbagbo made his case for a "democratic alternative," the Ivorian president's claim that his rule had been beneficial for the country's economic and social development was under severe strain. Côte d'Ivoire was facing an increasingly grave economic crisis, which gave the impetus to and opened up the space for political contestation. This situation was further aggravated by liberal internationalist interventionism in the Ivorian economy. The "rise of democracy" in the wake of the ending of the Cold War in Africa, meanwhile, piled further pressure on Houphouët-Boigny. But despite being increasingly frail and a target himself, he pragmatically and ruthlessly adapted to the new circumstances, came out again on top one last time, and prevented his house of cards from falling apart during his lifetime.

Côte d'Ivoire's economic miracle was not a mirage but a fair-weather construct, where the key players extracted resources when the sun was shining rather than saving in preparation for rainy days. As a result, when the Ivorian economy came to face strong international headwinds during the 1970s, its weaknesses and irregularities were increasingly exposed, and by the 1980s the situation had deteriorated significantly.

While the economic growth numbers still seemed encouraging during much of the 1970s, the global recession of that decade heavily affected Côte d'Ivoire by sending international commodity prices tumbling. The Agricultural Products Price Stabilization and Support Fund had—among other reasons—been put in place to protect Ivorian farmers from exactly these market price fluctuations. The sheer severity and continuity in the fall of prices, however, drained the fund and, relatedly, the country's financial resources. The problem was that the fund's reserves were clearly insufficient, not least because of poor management, corruption, and embezzlement. Moreover, the sense of security that the fund provided had encouraged overproduction, notably of cacao, which only further aggravated international price falls. Finally, Houphouët-Boigny did not hesitate to resort to the fund to finance major national infrastructure as well as vanity projects. Consequently, the country suffered from both a dramatic loss in export revenue and rising debt.

With agriculture being the heart and lungs of the Ivorian economy, the still relatively small industrial sector was not in a position to offer any compensation, especially because it had its own problems. Still largely concentrated in Abidjan and in foreign hands, it could and would not provide a solution in the national interest, and suffered from increased production costs through skyrocketing energy prices, falling domestic demand, and lack of capital. In 1980 alone, the country's GDP thus contracted by a dramatic 11 percent,[16] and GDP per capita fell even further, by a whopping 14.3 percent.[17]

Only two decades into independence, the International Monetary Fund (IMF) thus felt compelled to step in and bail out Houphouët-Boigny's Côte d'Ivoire. Inevitably, however, the financial lifeline came with strings attached, ranging from restructuring to austerity measures. The IMF's 1981 structural adjustment plan pushed for further liberalization and privatization, less subsidies, more taxes, and, importantly, a reduction in government spending. This brought the Ivorians only more immediate pain for supposedly long-term gain. The reduction in benefits for such public sector employees as teachers, meanwhile, provoked hitherto unseen demonstrations and led to large-scale strikes by students, teachers, and civil servants, particularly in Abidjan.

Although this was an unprecedented situation for Houphouët-Boigny, he succeeded in restoring order by using a combination of his tested methods of dialogue, concessions, and repression. But with fewer carrots available to secure compliance, the Ivorian president wielded the stick more strongly. Rather than suffering at the hands of the old sage's henchmen, some of his major critics chose exile. This was the case of Gbagbo, who, as a member of the National Union of Research and

Higher Education (Syndicat national de la recherche et de l'enseignement supérieur, SYNARES), had gained a certain prominence in the demonstrations and strikes of early 1982.

Despite his strong hand and preemptive exile for opponents, Houphouët-Boigny did not succeed in totally silencing his critics, who secretly regrouped and, like Gbagbo, harangued him from the safe distance of the former metropole. It did certainly not help that the aging president seemed to be increasingly out of touch with his own people, who after the miracle years of rising living standards were facing economic recession, restructuring, and austerity. Instead of showing restraint, he plowed on with building himself a monument by transforming Yamoussoukro into the capital of Côte d'Ivoire. The splurging of vast sums on what seemed like an unnecessary folly while people had to tighten their belts raised more than an eyebrow. While not accepting the increasing dysfunctionality of his regime and rule, the Ivorian leader nevertheless felt compelled to explain himself. In spring 1983, faced with a renewed teachers' strike, he claimed, in a rather elaborate way, that he had paid with his own money for the transformation of Yamoussoukro. Yet instead of assuaging concerns about the misappropriation of government funds, in making his point he bizarrely flaunted his enormous wealth, "billions" that he held in his "bank accounts, in Switzerland."[18] Meanwhile, he indirectly laid the blame for the agitation on foreign communist interference and sponsorship, because Côte d'Ivoire was "considered the anti-communist stronghold to be destroyed."[19]

Houphouët-Boigny continued to play his anti-communist tune not only to discredit his critics, but also to retain Western—notably financial—support, to tighten his grip on the PDCI, and to retain one-party rule. This was all clearly on display at his party's congress in October 1985. In the monumental and largely unfiltered press conference he gave afterwards, he emphasized the importance of unity, warned against ethnic division, and explained that the constitution had "planned for multipartyism . . . once the conditions were in place. For the moment," he observed, "they are not."[20] The concentration of power in one party and, ultimately, one man had raised the question of succession since the early days of the Republic of Côte d'Ivoire. But Houphouët-Boigny repetitively refrained from settling the question, even though it became ever more pressing the older he got. The question thus came up again at the post-PDCI congress press conference. Although he was now, at least according to his official birthday, eighty years old, he remained evasive. Instead of providing clarity, he indirectly applauded himself that unlike other African heads of state he did not pass on power to his children: "I have been in politics for two generations of Houphouëts. I am therefore much freer to choose with complete peace of mind the profile of the person who will ensure continuity."[21]

In light of his advanced age and deteriorating health, having been diagnosed with prostate cancer five years earlier, he was probably overly optimistic about the time remaining at his disposal to make a decision about his succession. The global and African context and mood, meanwhile, became increasingly less accommodating to dictatorial rule, however enlightened and pro-Western. With the winding down of the Cold War in Africa in the late 1980s, Houphouët-Boigny's anti-communist narrative went out of fashion, and the international voices for democratization to follow economic liberalist intervention grew louder. Moreover, the economic woes had not gone away, and the various measures to redress the Ivorian economy while assuring political stability ultimately backfired. By 1990, the situation reached a boiling point, which, on the one hand, forced the aging despot's hand but, on the other, demonstrated that by opening up the political system to other parties and laying down the rules for succession, he remained in control of Côte d'Ivoire.

In March 1990, anonymous tracts began to circulate in Abidjan that directly attacked Houphouët-Boigny—specifically in relation to his personal wealth—and called for demonstrations against him and his regime. These calls fell on fertile ground, and Abidjan and other Ivorian cities rapidly became engulfed in major demonstrations. What increasingly amounted to a popular pro-democracy uprising was led and reinforced by the unions, which called for and went on ever more far-reaching strikes. The most radical and determined among these groups was the research and higher-education union SYNARES, which, joined by students and teachers, brought the educational sector to a standstill. Initially, the regime responded by staging counterprotests, selectively arresting ringleaders, and using force to prevent or at least limit the demonstrations. The resulting clashes between protesters and the regime's supporters and security forces eventually led to casualties that, combined with international pressure, fears for reputational damage, and the devastating economic effects of the strikes, led to a rethink in the presidential palace. In April, the Ivorian government opened the door to multipartyism by recognizing the Ivorian Popular Front (Front populaire ivoirien, FPI), which Gbagbo—who had been graciously allowed to return from Paris a few years earlier—had secretly founded with his wife, Simone, in exile. This was followed the same month by the recognition of another political formation, the Ivorian Workers' Party (Parti ivoirien des travailleurs, PIT).

Since Houphouët-Boigny's PDCI-RDA had been a very broad, if not the only, political "church" in Côte d'Ivoire and was worn-out after three decades in power, it began to hemorrhage members to the new political formations. Moreover, it was divided into factions following the emergence of the "Reformers" (Rénovateurs), who wanted to liberalize and modernize the party and country in a hardly veiled attack on Houphouëtism. In light of this internal division and external competition his party now faced, it was not a foregone conclusion that the old sage would be re-elected in the presidential elections of October 1990. But despite now being eighty-five, Houphouët-Boigny rose to the occasion and threw all he had into the political battle. Likely resorting to manipulation and outright cheating, he eventually won the elections with 82 percent of the vote, while Gbagbo gained 18 percent. By objective standards, this was a clear result and endorsement for the Ivorian leader. But it was unlikely to represent the true voting intentions of the Ivorian people and stood obviously in contrast to the 100 percent he had obtained five years earlier. Côte d'Ivoire was not anymore entirely "his" country.

In extending the life of his regime, Houphouët-Boigny not only modified the political system, but also made pragmatic changes to his regime. Simultaneous with opening up the political stage to other parties in spring 1990, he appointed Alassane Ouattara as president of the Interministerial Committee for the Coordination of the Economic Stabilization and Recovery Program to, as the committee's name indicates, bring the country's economic situation under control and to please his international donors, the IMF, and the World Bank. An Ivorian with a distinguished career at the IMF and governor of the Central Bank of West African States (Banque centrale des États de l'Afrique de l'Ouest, BCEAO) at the time of his appointment, Ouattara brought the obvious experience and skill set, as well as the trust of the international backers, to the position. Moreover, the international civil servant and development economist did not seem to have any political aspirations that could pose a threat to Houphouët-Boigny's rule.

Therefore, visibly satisfied with Ouattara's initial performance, the Ivorian president, after his reelection, appointed him as his first-ever prime minister in a constitutional novelty in November. This quasi-revolutionary change to the structure and functioning of the regime then finally convinced the Ivorian leader of the need to regulate his succession. The constitutional reforms thus also included an article clarifying that in the case of the president's death, incapacity, or resignation, the president of the National Assembly, who at the time was Côte d'Ivoire's former first ambassador to the United States and minister of the economy and finance Henri Konan Bédié, would take over as interim president.

Despite clarifying his succession and—at least theoretically—opening up the Ivorian political system, Houphouët-Boigny and his government remained confronted with criticism and opposition. Although Ouattara managed to balance the books, the additional austerity measures required to achieve this inevitably proved unpopular with large segments of the Ivorian population. This resulted in renewed flare-ups of strikes and demonstrations, wherein the youth, especially the students who had regrouped within the Student and School Federation of Côte d'Ivoire (Fédération estudiantine et scolaire de Côte d'Ivoire, FESCI), played an increasingly prominent role. The regime, which, other than abdicating, had exhausted its peaceful means to calm the situation, did not tolerate the student protests and eventually cracked down on them with its security forces, including army units led by Colonel Robert Guéï.

Meanwhile, the PDCI-RDA was challenged not only by the Reformers, but also by factionalism between the Bédiéistes and the Alassanistes, who supported the president of the National Assembly and the prime minister, respectively. Notwithstanding the Ivorian president's succession ruling and initial impression of Ouattara as lacking any political ambitions, the prime minister developed an appetite for power. But despite his competence, the fact that he was seen by many as an outsider imposed on the country by the international financial donors, and accusations that he was a foreigner because of his father's Burkinabe roots, limited his appeal within the party and with the Ivorian people. The Bédié faction, meanwhile, saw the legitimacy of the constitutional ruling on the succession questioned. These issues were amplified in the now free Ivorian press, wherein the opposition attacked both of the two potential heirs of Houphouët-Boigny.

The jostling within the PDCI-RDA and between parties in Côte d'Ivoire was fueled by a certain sense of urgency because even the old sage was not immortal, and it became increasingly obvious in the early 1990s that he was about to leave the stage. In June 1993, his advanced age and cancer forced him to undergo a prostate operation, for which he chose the Cochin Hospital in Paris. The intervention bought him some time, but in

October he had again to be admitted to the same hospital. Once stabilized, he then went to rest in Geneva, Switzerland. The stay at the clinic there was cut short, however, because it became instantly obvious that he was rapidly nearing his end. He was thus flown in all urgency back home to Yamoussoukro, where he arrived on 19 November to spend his final days among his loved ones. On 7 December, he passed away.

His long-awaited yet expected death immediately prompted the Bédiéistes into action. Fearful of an Alassaniste seizure of power, within hours of Houphouët-Boigny's death Bédié marched, flanked by soldiers, into the state television station and announced his succession himself rather than waiting on the country's institutions to do it for him. This sense of urgency was probably misplaced, because the French, who were the ultimate arbiters in Ivorian politics, preferred Bédié over Ouattara, whom they saw as "America's man" because of his years of service in US-dominated international financial institutions. Outpaced by Bédié, and without a constitutional case or French support, the prime minister resigned on 9 December.

The succession had thus been resolved—at least temporarily—when Côte d'Ivoire's first president and ruler of more than three decades was laid to rest. Following a period of official mourning in January 1994, which gave Ivorians the opportunity to pay tribute to their leader and extend their sympathy to his family, a gigantic state funeral was held from 2 to 7 February in both Abidjan and Yamoussoukro. The closing ceremony was attended by almost everyone of rank and name in Africa, both past and present, with a veritable parade of heads of state, ranging from close allies such as Gabon's Bongo to more ambivalent partners like Zaïre's Mobutu.

FIGURE 4.2. With François Mitterrand, 1980s. Courtesy of Fondation Félix Houphouët-Boigny.

Reflecting Houphouët-Boigny's importance for postcolonial Africa, his funeral even brought together sworn enemies of past adventures, notably Gowon and Ojukwu, the former leaders of Nigeria and Biafra, respectively. But the most significant delegation was probably the French one. In addition to President Mitterrand (see figure 4.2), who in the early 1950s had sealed the Ivorian leader's original alliance with France, the French delegation consisted of—among others—his predecessor Valéry Giscard d'Estaing, de Gaulle's oldest son Admiral Philippe de Gaulle, mayor of Paris and future president Jacques Chirac, former prime minister Debré, and, of course, Foccart. Not only had Houphouët-Boigny been one of them, but it was also clear that Paris was holding on to Côte d'Ivoire and its sphere of influence despite the death of "France's man in Africa."

Conclusion

As Houphouët-Boigny was laid to rest in early 1994, the large French funeral contingent led by Mitterrand was a visible testimony to his decades-long proximity to and collaboration with France, as well as the French determination to retain Côte d'Ivoire and its sphere of influence in francophone Africa. In criticizing the Ivorian leader as "the most conscious resistance to the evolution and liberation of Africa" in 1960, the revolutionary Frantz Fanon thus had a point and demonstrated foresight, particularly regarding the "full" decolonization of Africa. Although Houphouët-Boigny eventually accepted the fate of independence and even ostentatiously went for a clean break with the metropole, immediately afterwards he formalized a neocolonial relationship with Paris. On this basis, he then colluded with the French to help them safeguard their political, economic, and strategic interests in Côte d'Ivoire and francophone Africa, as well as to reach beyond their usual sphere of influence on the continent. Working and conspiring hand in hand with his ally and friend Foccart to establish a *pax gallica,* the Ivorian president seemed indeed to be "France's man in Africa."

Born in the heyday of French colonialism in Africa into Baoulé nobility, Houphouët-Boigny was rapidly sucked into France's imperial project. After successfully completing the educational *cursus honorum* that took him from his village, Yamoussoukro, to the capital of French West Africa, Dakar, he then served the colonial apparatus first as an African doctor and then as cantonal chief in Côte d'Ivoire. In the wake of the Second World War, he was elected to represent his colony in the French National Assembly of the Fourth Republic, became part of successive iterations of its government during the 1950s, and contributed to and supported France's two major attempts to salvage its empire, first Defferre's *loi-cadre* and then especially de Gaulle's Community. When he acceded to the highest office of independent Côte d'Ivoire in 1960, before the emergence of the neocolonial collusion later described as *Françafrique,* he had already served France for decades. Yet inasmuch as he had been an agent of French colonialism, he had also been both a victim and critic of colonialism.

In his various postings as an African doctor during the interwar period, he not only suffered unequal treatment by his French superiors but also witnessed the inequality that existed throughout Côte d'Ivoire. Initially, he largely swallowed this unfairness while trying to build a career and life. But when the injustice hit closer to home, notably at a time when he became increasingly involved in his family's plantation, he chose to challenge the colonial authorities. Confronted with the discrimination faced by African planters in what was still a medical posting, he experimented for the first time with unionism, albeit to no avail. After having experienced Vichy's escalating wartime oppression as a major African planter, however, he established with his peers the SAA to challenge the supremacy of French over African farmers. With this union and the arrival of more benevolent colonial authorities towards the war's end, he then succeeded in redressing many of the inequalities Ivorian planters like him had been facing.

It was based on this local success that he then launched his political career proper, which, after the war, led him to the newly constituted French parliament in Paris. There he continued his struggle for African emancipation at an imperial level and almost instantly rose to prominence through his major role in the abolition of forced labor in the colonies. Building on this momentum and his African planters union, he then launched a political party, the PDCI, in Côte d'Ivoire, and a regional movement, the RDA, of which his party became a branch as the PDCI-RDA. Riding a wave of success, he found the winds rapidly turning against him. His fight for African emancipation proved too much of a challenge for France's colonial order, and with the onset of the Cold War, his affiliation with the French communists singled him and his party out as targets. In the late 1940s, he and especially his comrades and followers, who unlike him were not protected by parliamentary immunity, suffered under an unprecedented crackdown by the colonial authorities.

Colonial repression could have ended Houphouët-Boigny's political ambitions or forced him to opt for violent struggle. But instead, in a dramatic demonstration of his pragmatism and ability to adapt to new circumstances, if not to seize new opportunities, he broke with the communists and aligned himself with the French political establishment through Mitterrand and his Democratic and Socialist Union of the Resistance. This was the real beginning of his alliance with France, which allowed him during the 1950s to have an increasingly free rein in Ivorian politics and to influence the development of the French empire in line with his and his country's interests. The implosion of the Community, however, forced him again to adapt. In what amounted to an audacious challenge to de Gaulle, he succeeded in almost instantly and temporarily reinventing himself as an African nationalist and obtained from France independence without strings attached, and then tailor-made cooperation agreements for Côte d'Ivoire and its Entente allies. He did not lose his opportunistic ability, even in old age. When the economic and political order in his country began to unravel at the end of the Cold War, he drew in external resources, reformed the political system and his regime, and, when deemed necessary, used force to maintain order.

The Ivorian leader was no stranger to the use of force. Early on in his rule, he unleashed waves of repression in response to alleged but ultimately inexistent conspiracies in order to make his regime bulletproof in a hostile regional environment shaken by coups. In cracking down and shaking the Ivorian people to their core, he counted on French support. In relying on the secret Franco-Ivorian domestic security deal, the driving force in this neocolonial collusion was Houphouët-Boigny, and not the Élysée. Although the Ivorian president, at least initially, enabled and assisted French efforts towards establishing a *pax gallica* in the region, this pattern—of pursuing and at times initiating his own agenda—was mirrored in how he engaged and meddled in African affairs. Moreover, the main cause of his insecurity at home was also what initially drove him in his African policy, namely his fear of and rivalry with Nkrumah.

The sportsmanlike competition between the Ivorian and Ghanaian leaders rapidly turned sour. With independence, Accra's indirect support to the separatist aspirations of the Sanwi in Côte d'Ivoire, and the arrival and escalation of the Cold War in Africa, they became enemies who sought backing in the opposing moderate Monrovia and radical Casablanca blocs. In response to what he perceived as the mounting, radical, and Soviet-sponsored Ghanaian threat, Houphouët-Boigny wanted to strengthen and maintain France's protection of his country, regime, and especially himself. This transformed Abidjan into a French stronghold and the nerve center for implementing the Élysée's neo-imperial policies in Africa, with the Ivorian president joining forces with Foccart to expand France's regional influence, notably in the Congo. The Ivorian leader was not, however, a mere neocolonial stooge. As illustrated by his Biafran crusade and policy of dialogue with South Africa, in pursuit of his own regional ambitions and Cold War agenda, he forced France into action, carried other African allies with him, and if necessary did not hesitate to go it alone.

In addition to France's actual or at least tacit support, the reason Houphouët-Boigny could embark on his foreign adventures without fearing a domestic backlash that might endanger him and his regime was that he sat safely in the saddle back home. In combination with repressive warning shots in the early independence years and sporadic bouts of repression thereafter, he also enabled phenomenal economic growth that improved the living conditions of Ivorians. The sticks were thus accompanied by what seemed to be a never-ending supply of carrots. The problem was that with an overwhelming focus on agriculture, fair-weather economic and financial instruments, mismanagement, and corruption, the supply of carrots dried out. This became even more problematic when Côte d'Ivoire had to be bailed out by the IMF, and ordinary Ivorians were forced to tighten their belts while their leader shelled out money on megalomaniac projects like transforming Yamoussoukro into the capital, accompanied by a basilica that overshadowed the Vatican. Despite his claim that "the happiness of the Ivorian people" was his "only goal," throughout his life he also ruthlessly pursued his self-interest, whether to benefit himself as an African planter, to save his skin from colonial persecution, to regain the political upper hand, or simply to enrich himself. Nevertheless, he was aware that his popularity and authority with the Ivorian people were important because what made him so valuable for France in the first place was his African leadership credentials that he had originally earned by challenging the French empire. Houphouët-Boigny was neither a freedom fighter nor a collaborator in the conventional sense, but a figure who defied binary classifications, charted his own course, and became one of the most influential African leaders of the postcolonial era.

Notes

Introduction

Epigraph: "Houphouët-Boigny est objectivement le frein le plus conscient à l'évolution et à la libération de l'Afrique." Frantz Fanon, *Pour la révolution africaine: Écrits politiques* (Editions La Découverte, 2006), 203.

1. This term is commonly used by commentators to describe the official and unofficial networks that formed the foundation of the neocolonial relationship between France and its former colonies in the postindependence era. Tony Chafer, "*Françafrique,*" in *Routledge Handbook of Francophone Africa,* ed. Tony Chafer and Margaret A. Majumdar (Routledge, 2023).
2. Pierre Nandjui, *Houphouët-Boigny: L'homme de la France en Afrique* (L'Harmattan, 1995).
3. Antoine Glaser, *AfricaFrance: Quand les dirigeants africains deviennent les maîtres du jeu* (Librairie Arthème Fayard / Pluriel, 2017).
4. Aristide R. Zolberg, *One-Party Government in the Ivory Coast,* 2nd ed. (Princeton University Press, 1969), viii.
5. Frédéric Grah Mel, *Félix Houphouët-Boigny,* 3 vols. (Editions du CERAP and Maisonneuve et Larose, 2003–10).

6. Paul-Henri Siriex, *Félix Houphouët-Boigny: L'homme de la paix* (Nouvelles Éditions Africaines, 1975); Paul-Henri Siriex, *Houphouët-Boigny ou la sagesse africaine* (Éditions Nathan and Nouvelles Éditions Africaines, 1986).

Chapter 1: The Making of a Leader

Epigraph: "On a en effet beaucoup écrit sur moi, de très belles choses. S'il y a eu des erreurs, elles n'ont pas été commises de mauvaise foi, mais dans l'ignorance des faits et de la nature même de notre société à nous." Félix Houphouët-Boigny, *Mes premiers combats,* ed. Patrice Vautier (Edition°1 and Nouvelles Éditions Ivoiriennes, 1994), 15.

1. The Brazzaville Conference (30 January–8 February 1944), convened by de Gaulle and his Free French, aimed to secure the loyalty of France's African colonies by rejecting independence but proposing reforms for greater autonomy, economic development, and political representation, reflecting a strategic effort to maintain colonial control while addressing growing demands for change.
2. "Indignation chez les Européens: je les accusais pratiquement de génocide." Houphouët-Boigny, *Mes premiers combats,* 60.
3. Quoted in F. O. Alalade, "President Felix Houphouet-Boigny, the Ivory Coast, and France," *Journal of African Studies* 6, no. 3 (1979): 122.
4. Laurent Gbagbo, *La Côte d'Ivoire: Économie et société à la veille de l'indépendance (1940–1960)* (L'Harmattan, 1982), 6.
5. "J'étais à cette époque dans une situation de véritable désarroi: ma mère, mon frère et mon fils aîné avaient disparu. Ma seule ambition était de me

consacrer aux affaires de mon petit canton. Celles du pays, à d'autres!" Houphouët-Boigny, *Mes premiers combats,* 87.

6. "Mme Denise Gadeau: Ce n'était pas un patron commode," in Frédéric Grah Mel, *Rencontres avec Félix Houphouët-Boigny* (Frat Mat Editions, 2005), 63.
7. "De toute part, je fus sollicité pour me présenter au second collège." Houphouët-Boigny, *Mes premiers combats,* 95.
8. Siriex, *Félix Houphouët-Boigny,* 60.
9. "C'est en hommes libres que nous entendons entrer librement dans l'Union française. Or, nous ne sommes pas tous libres. Le travail forcé, cette survivance de la corvée autrefois si décriée en France, auquel nous demeurons assujettis, fera de nous des esclaves dans l'Union, s'il n'est pas aboli au préalable. Il ne saurait y avoir dans l'Union française des maîtres et des esclaves, mais des aînés et des cadets d'une même et grande famille, des cadets respectueux de l'âge, reconnaissants des services rendus, des aînés soucieux de faire rattraper aux cadets l'avance prise sur eux dans le difficile chemin de la liberté et de la civilisation. . . . Les plantations, aussi, peuvent vivre avec la suppression radicale et immédiate du travail forcé. Ce n'est pas . . . un démagogue qui vous parle. C'est un gros propriétaire terrien qui a librement renoncé au travail forcé, un homme qui vit avec sa nombreuse famille exclusivement de cette exploitation, un homme que plus de 12000 de ses camarades ont choisi pour présider le seul grand groupement agricole existant en Afrique noire française, un homme qui, s'il était un démagogue, risquerait de précipiter dans la misère des centaines et des centaines de braves cultivateurs qui ont placé

toute leur confiance en lui. Nous demeurons fermement convaincus que, si les colons payent bien la main-d'œuvre et surtout la traitent mieux, ils pourront maintenir non seulement leur production, mais même l'accroître." "Rapport sur la suppression du travail forcé dans les territoires d'outre-mer, Assemblée nationale constituante, 30 mars 1946," in Félix Houphouët-Boigny, *Anthologie des discours 1946–1978,* vol. 1, *Du 30 mars 1946 au 4 janvier 1963* (Céda, 1978), 25, 37.

Chapter 2: African Nationalist *Malgré Lui*

Epigraph: "J'ai attendu la fiancée sur le parvis de l'église, un bouquet à la main. La fiancée n'est pas venue. Les fleurs se sont fanées." Jacques Foccart, *Foccart Parle,* interviews by Philippe Gaillard (Fayard / Jeune Afrique, 1995), 1:199.

1. *Eurafrique* refers to the concept of fostering a close economic, political, and cultural partnership between Europe and Africa. It was framed during the interwar years but revived in the postwar period as a way to integrate Africa's resources and labor into Europe's development while maintaining a hierarchical relationship that favored European interests.
2. "Les jeunes n'imaginent pas aujourd'hui à quel point la police nous harcelait quand le RDA a commencé la politique. Nous étions perquisitionnés tous les jours. On fouillait nos affaires." "Mme Denise Gadeau," in Grah Mel, *Rencontres,* 63.
3. "Nous devrions présenter un front commun afin de faire aboutir nos revendications. Alors qu'ouvriers socialistes et communistes sont solidaires dans leurs justes revendications, alors qu'élus socialistes

et communistes desserviraient la classe ouvrière, qui est une, s'ils ne résistaient pas ensemble aux forces de la réaction, l'administration réactionnaire coloniale fait de l'anticommunisme outre-mer, afin de dresser les uns contre les autres les démocrates africains." Félix Houphouët-Boigny, "Le continent africain en marche, 'Réveil' de Dakar—décembre 1947," in Houphouët-Boigny, *Anthologie des discours,* 1:55.

4. The collective body of government ministers chaired by the prime minister and responsible for executive decision-making.
5. "Le R.D.A. peut beaucoup dans ce pays: il peut et doit rapprocher les hommes de bonne volonté, quelle que soit leur idéologie politique, pour la réalisation en commun d'un programme de progrès économique et social dans l'intérêt supérieur de la Côte d'Ivoire, de la France et de l' Union française. Nous nous sommes rendu compte que notre apparentement au groupe communiste était, dans une certaine mesure, un empêchement à ce rapprochement. . . . Nous avons quitté l'apparentement d'avec le groupe communiste. Nous avons voté et continuons à voter la confiance aux gouvernements. . . . Nous n'avons jamais partagé l'idéologie communiste. Mais il est clair que notre action parlementaire . . . serait vaine si dans un territoire comme la Côte d'Ivoire dont l'immense majorité nous fait confiance . . . , nous ne réussissions à collaborer avec tous ceux, Blancs et Noirs, qui, comme nous, ont un intérêt primordial à voir ce territoire, aux possibilités infinies, s'engager résolument dans la voie du progrès économique et social." "Solennelle déclaration publique au Stade Géo André à

Abidjan, 6 octobre 1951," in Houphouët-Boigny, *Anthologie des discours*, 1:84–86.

6. "Vous balkanisez l'Afrique, vous allez à l'encontre de son aspiration à l'unité." Quoted in Pierre Messmer, "1958–1960: Du rêve à la réalité . . . ," in *Léopold Sédar Senghor: La pensée et l'action politique; Actes du colloque organisé par la section française de l'Assemblée parlementaire de la Francophonie* (Assemblée Nationale and Organisation Internationale de la Francophonie, 2006), 96.
7. Pierre Messmer, *Les blancs s'en vont: Récits de décolonisation* (Albin Michel, 1998), 87.
8. Félix Houphouët-Boigny, "Black Africa and the French Union," *Foreign Affairs* 35, no. 4 (1957): 593, 598.
9. Norland (Abidjan) to US Department of State, 16 December 1956, National Archives and Records Administration, College Park, MD, RG 84, Entry 2820-C, Box 2.
10. Guéna (Abidjan) to Foccart (Communauté), 19 October 1960, Archives Nationales, Pierrefitte-sur-Seine, Archives du secrétariat général des Affaires africaines et malgaches de la Communauté (5 AG F)/530 (hereafter AN, 5 AG F).

Chapter 3: "Cold" Warrior

Epigraph: "Or la Côte d'Ivoire est très anticommuniste. En effet, le nationalisme ivoirien existe et c'est une chance car l'Ivoirien est un cultivateur. Il vit de son sol et vit très bien grâce à lui. Il est donc attaché à son sol, donc à son pays. Il est prêt à défendre son bien contre le communisme. La Côte d'Ivoire est un pays riche, il lui faut simplement prendre conscience de cette situation et l'Ivoirien tout naturellement sera anti-communiste." Procès Verbal du Comité de Défense réuni le 26 septembre 1961 à 17 heures, à la Présidence de la République, 26 September 1961, AN, 5 AG F/1787.

1. "Croyez-vous . . . ces milliards que notre grand ami Kwamé N'Krumah engagera dans une organisation militaire vont servir à quelque chose, sinon au faux prestige? . . . Kwamé N'Krumah peut-il vraiment attaquer un territoire quelconque s'il en avait l'intention? Je ne crois pas." "Discours prononcé au Stade Géo-André, 7 septembre 1958," in Houphouët-Boigny, *Anthologie des discours,* 1:203–4.
2. "régime fantoche." "La République Démocratique du Congo," in Arsène Assouan Usher, *La République de Côte d'Ivoire au service de l'Afrique et de la paix* (Delroisse, 1966), 109.
3. "Nous voulons la paix au Congo. Il faut dépersonnaliser les problèmes. Quel que soit l'homme au pouvoir au Congo, nous devons considérer, à partir du moment où nous avons accepté librement la Charte de l'O.U.A. à Addis-Abéba, charte dont les principes essentiels se résument en ceci: égalité absolue de tous les pays membres, respect de la souveraineté des Etats membres, non immixtion dans les affaires intérieures de chaque pays—à partir du moment où nous avons accepté cela librement, notre devoir est de respecter scrupuleusement les bases de cette charte." "Discours prononcé á Korhogo, 7 mai 1965," in Félix Houphouët-Boigny, *Anthologie des discours 1946–1978,* vol. 2, *Du 16 février 1963 au 9 février 1971* (Céda, 1978), 654.
4. "Il va certes de l'intérêt du Biafra, mais aussi de l'avenir de l'ensemble africain, qu'une politique aveugle pratiquée par les alliés anglo-saxons de la France risque

de jeter dans une situation extrêmement dangereuse avec la maléfique influence à terme des arabes révolutionnaires d'Algérie et d'Egypte et de l'implantation de leurs alliés communistes russes et chinois au cœur de ce continent où jusqu'ici, chrétiens, animistes et musulmans ont vécu en excellentes termes, en collaboration fraternelle." Houphouët-Boigny to de Gaulle, 24 July 1968, AN, 5 AG F/535.

5. "Nos relations avec des pays où sévit la discrimination raciale contribuent incontestablement à la réalisation progressive de l'égalité raciale. On découvre en nous d'autres nègres, d'autres hommes, des hommes comme les autres hommes, et c'est heureux." "Discours prononcé au Ve Congrès du Parti démocratique de Côte d'Ivoire, 30 octobre 1970," in Houphouët-Boigny, *Anthologie des discours,* 2:1075.

Chapter 4: Enlightened Despot

Epigraph: "Le bonheur de l'homme ivoirien est notre seul but, n'avons-nous jamais cessé de proclamer." "Discours prononcé devant l'Assemblée constituante pour la présentation du budget 1960, 31 décembre 1959," in Houphouët-Boigny, *Anthologie des discours,* 1:316.

1. "Le dialogue est l'arme des forts et non des faibles, c'est l'arme de ceux qui font passer les problèmes généraux avant les problems particuliers, avant les questions d'amour-propre. Dans la recherche de la paix, de la vraie paix, de la paix juste et durable on ne doit pas hésiter un seul instant, à recouvrir, avec obstination au dialogue." Félix Houphouët-Boigny, *Le Petit livre vert du Président de la République: Un Sage a dit . . . ; Recueil des pensées du Président Houphouët-Boigny* (Ministère de l'Information, 1974), 54.

2. Abou B. Bamba, *African Miracle, African Mirage: Transnational Politics and the Paradox of Modernization in Ivory Coast* (Ohio University Press, 2016).
3. "Article 3.—Sur demande du Président de la République de Côte d'Ivoire adressée à l'Ambassadeur de la République française une aide peut être fournie au Gouvernement de Côte d'Ivoire notamment sous forme de soutien logistique et de transmissions, par les forces armées françaises dans la mesure de leurs moyens et en l'absence de moyens correspondants de la République de Côte d'Ivoire. . . . Article 4.—Devant une situation particulièrement grave, le Président de la République de Côte d'Ivoire peut demander à titre exceptionnel l'intervention des forces armées françaises dans les formes prévues à l'Annexe I de la présente Convention." Convention spéciale sur les conditions de participation eventuelle des Forces armées françaises au maintien de l'ordre public sur le territoire de la République de Côte d'Ivoire, Annexes, I–IV, Michel Debré and Félix Houphouët-Boigny, 9 February 1962, Service historique de la Défense, Vincennes, GR 1 S 153.
4. "Le Président Houphouët-Boigny compte faire une demande précise au Général de Gaulle pour que le concours ou tout au moins la 'présence' de l'armée française lui soit assurée lors des quelques jours tendus qu'il craint devoir vivre." Note, Raphaël-Leygues, 6 August 1963, AN, 5 AG F/535.
5. "Un miracle, comme un pari, cela se prépare, cela se conditionne, cela se mesure, cela se décide et cela se réalise à force de volonté et de persévérance." Félix Houphouët-Boigny, *Textes de référence* (Fraternité Hebdo éditions, 1980), 64.

6. "Il n'y a pas de miracle ivoirien. D'ailleurs, à l'opposé, certains ont parlé de mirage. Il n'y a ni mirage ni miracle. Il y a le fruit de l'effort de tout un peuple uni, au sein de notre grand Parti le PDCI-RDA, avec le seul souci de nous sortir du carcan de dépendance économique." "En matière économique, le miracle n'est que la conséquence d'une bonne gestion." Houphouët-Boigny, *Textes de référence*, 65.
7. Grah Mel, *Félix Houphouët-Boigny*, vol. 2, *L'épreuve du pouvoir (1960–1980)* (Editions du CERAP and Karthala, 2010), 339.
8. "GDP Growth (Annual %)—Côte d'Ivoire," World Bank Group, accessed 2 March 2026, https://data.worldbank.org/indicator/NY.GDP.MKTP.KD.ZG?locations=CI.
9. "Population Growth in Ivory Coast," WorldData.info, last modified January 2026, https://www.worlddata.info/africa/ivory-coast/populationgrowth.php.
10. "GDP per Capita Growth (Annual %)—Côte d'Ivoire," World Bank Group, accessed 2 March 2026, https://data.worldbank.org/indicator/NY.GDP.PCAP.KD.ZG?locations=CI.
11. "GDP Growth (Annual %)—Ghana," World Bank Group, accessed 2 March 2026, https://data.worldbank.org/indicator/NY.GDP.MKTP.KD.ZG?locations=GH.
12. "GDP per Capita Growth (Annual %)—Ghana," World Bank Group, accessed 2 March 2026, https://data.worldbank.org/indicator/NY.GDP.PCAP.KD.ZG?locations=GH.
13. Beth S. Rabinowitz, *Coups, Rivals, and the Modern State: Why Rural Coalitions Matter in Sub-Saharan Africa* (Cambridge University Press, 2018), 159.
14. "Le bilan de la gestion de notre pays par un homme, Houphouët-Boigny; par un parti, le P.D.C.I. Un

mot caractérise ce bilan: dictature. Dictature personnelle d'un individu appuyé sur ce parti unique de godillots." Laurent Gbagbo, *Côte d'Ivoire: Pour une alternative démocratique* (L'Harmattan, 1983), 7.

15. Gbagbo, *Pour une alternative démocratique*, 9–10.
16. "GDP Growth (Annual %)—Côte d'Ivoire."
17. "GDP per Capita Growth (Annual %)—Côte d'Ivoire."
18. "Autrefois, on recevait très peu, peut-être cent millions de francs, mais ces cent millions valent aujourd'hui des milliards. Et j'ai viré tout cet argent dans mes comptes en banque, en Suisse, et cela a produit des intérêts importants." Félix Houphouët-Boigny, "J'ai des milliards en Suisse . . . ," *Peuples noirs, peuples africains* 7, nos. 41–42 (1984): 97.
19. "Aujourd'hui la Côte-d'Ivoire est considérée comme le bastion anticommuniste à détruire." Houphouët-Boigny, "J'ai des milliards," 99.
20. "Dans notre Constitution, nous avons prévu le multipartisme. Il pourra s'établir quand les conditions seront créées. Pour le moment, elles ne le sont pas." Félix Houphouët-Boigny, *Conférence de presse du 14 octobre 1985* (Service de presse de la Présidence de la République, 1985), 54.
21. "J'ai fait la politique pour deux générations d'Houphouët. Je suis donc beaucoup plus libre pour choisir en toute quiétude le profil de celui qui assumera la continuité." Houphouët-Boigny, *Conférence de presse*, 7.

Bibliography

Published Documents

Fanon, Frantz. *Pour la révolution africaine: Écrits politiques.* Editions La Découverte, 2006.

Houphouët-Boigny, Félix. *Anthologie des discours 1946–1978.* 4 vols. Céda, 1978.

Houphouët-Boigny, Félix. "Black Africa and the French Union." *Foreign Affairs* 35, no. 4 (1957): 593–99.

Houphouët-Boigny, Félix. *Conférence de presse du 14 octobre 1985.* Service de presse de la Présidence de la République, 1985.

Houphouët-Boigny, Félix. "J'ai des milliards en Suisse . . ." *Peuples noirs, peuples africains* 7, nos. 41–42 (1984): 76–104.

Houphouët-Boigny, Félix. *Le Petit livre vert du Président de la République: Un Sage a dit . . . ; Recueil des pensées du Président Houphouët-Boigny.* Ministère de l'Information, 1974.

Houphouët-Boigny, Félix. *Textes de référence.* Fraternité Hebdo éditions, 1980.

Ministère des affaires etrangères. *La Côte d'Ivoire à l'Assemblée générale des Nations Unies 1960–1965.* Imprimerie Nationale, 1968.

Usher, Arsène Assouan. *La République de Côte d'Ivoire au service de l'Afrique et de la paix.* Delroisse, 1966.

Memoirs

Foccart, Jacques. *Foccart Parle.* Interviews by Philippe Gaillard. 2 vols. Fayard / Jeune Afrique, 1995, 1997.

Foccart, Jacques. *Journal de l'Elysée.* Edited by Philippe Gaillard. 3 vols. Fayard / Jeune Afrique, 1997–99.

Grah Mel, Frédéric. *Rencontres avec Félix Houphouët-Boigny.* Frat Mat Éditions, 2005.

Houphouët-Boigny, Félix. *Mes premiers combats.* Edited by Patrice Vautier. Édition°1 and Nouvelles Éditions Ivoiriennes, 1994.

Messmer, Pierre. *Les blancs s'en vont: Récits de décolonisation.* Albin Michel, 1998.

Soutou, Jean-Marie. *Un diplomate engagé: Mémoires 1939–1979.* Based on interviews by Jean-François Noiville. Introduction and notes by Georges-Henri Soutou. Editions de Fallois, 2011.

Secondary Sources

Aboussou, Dadoua. *Kwame Nkrumah and Félix Houphouët-Boigny: Divergent Perspectives on African Independence and Unity.* Cambridge Scholars Publishing, 2019.

Ageron, Charles-Robert, and Marc Michel, eds. *L'Afrique noire française: L'heure des indépendances.* CNRS Editions, 1992.

Ageron, Charles-Robert, and Marc Michel, eds. *L'Afrique noire française: L'heure des indépendances.* CNRS Editions, 2010.

Alalade, F. O. "President Felix Houphouet-Boigny, the Ivory Coast, and France." *Journal of African Studies* 6, no. 3 (1979): 122–131.

Aluko, Olajide. *The Foreign Policies of African States.* Hodder & Stoughton, 1977.

Amondji, Marcel. *Côte d'Ivoire: La dépendance et l'épreuve des faits.* L'Harmattan, 1988.
Amondji, Marcel. *Côte d'Ivoire: Le P.D.C.I. et la vie politique de 1944 à 1985.* L'Harmattan, 1986.
Amondji, Marcel. *Félix Houphouët et la Côte d'Ivoire: L'envers d'une légende.* Karthala, 1984.
Assouanga, Laurant, and Arthur Banga. "La construction d'un idéal national de paix: Analyse de l'action de Félix Houphouët-Boigny." *Identity, Culture and Politics* 19, nos. 1–2 (2018): 83–96.
Aworawo, David. "The Trajectory of Nigeria / Côte d'Ivoire Relations Since 1960." *Nigerian Journal of International Affairs* 37, no. 1 (2011): 1–26.
Bach, Daniel. "Le Général de Gaulle et la guerre civile au Nigeria." *Canadian Journal of African Studies / Revue canadienne des études africaines* 14, no. 2 (1980): 259–72.
Bach, Daniel. "L'insertion ivoirienne dans les rapports internationaux." *État et bourgeoisie en Côte d'Ivoire,* edited by Y.-A. Fauré and Jean-François Médard. Karthala, 1982.
Bach, Daniel. "Nigeria's Relations with France and Selected Francophone West African States, 1960–1975." PhD dissertation, University of Oxford, 1978.
Bailly, Diégou. *La restauration du multipartisme en Côte d'Ivoire ou la double mort d'Houphouët-Boigny.* L'Harmattan, 1995.
Bamba, Abou B. *African Miracle, African Mirage: Transnational Politics and the Paradox of Modernization in Ivory Coast.* Ohio University Press, 2016.
Bamba, Abou B. "An Unconventional Challenge to Apartheid: The Ivorian Dialogue Diplomacy with South Africa, 1960–1978." *International Journal of African Historical Studies* 47, no. 1 (2014): 77–99.

Banga, Arthur. "Civic Service and the Question of Extra-Military Missions of the Army in Franco-Ivorian Military Relations (1960–1970)." *International Journal of Military History and Historiography* 44, no. 2 (2024): 279–303.

Banga, Arthur. "L'aide militaire française dans la politique de défense de la Côte d'Ivoire de 1960 à 2002." PhD dissertation, Université Félix Houphouët-Boigny—Cocody and École Pratique des Hautes Études, 2014.

Banga, Arthur. "Le rôle des conseillers militaires français dans l'élaboration de l'outil de la défense ivoirienne de 1960 à 1980." In *Pratiques militaires et globalisation XIXe–XXIe siècles,* edited by Walter Bruyère-Ostells and François Dumasy. Bernard Giovanangeli éditeur, 2014.

Banga, Arthur. "Les armes: Un enjeu important des relations franco-ivoiriennes 1960–2015." *Stratégique,* no. 118 (2018): 139–54.

Banga, Arthur, and Camille Evrard. "La coopération militaire et les enjeux de défense en Afrique de l'Ouest: Le cas de la Mauritanie et de l'Entente." In Bat et al., *Jacques Foccart.*

Bat, Jean-Pierre. *La fabrique des "barbouzes": Histoire des réseaux Foccart en Afrique.* Nouveau Monde éditions, 2015.

Bat, Jean-Pierre. "Le rôle de la France après les indépendances: Jacques Foccart et la *pax gallica.*" *Afrique contemporaine,* no. 235 (2010): 43–52.

Bat, Jean-Pierre. *Le syndrome Foccart: La politique française en Afrique de 1959 à nos jours.* Gallimard, 2012.

Bat, Jean-Pierre, Olivier Forcade, and Sylvain Mary, eds. *Jacques Foccart: Archives ouvertes (1958–1974); La politique, l'Afrique et le monde.* Presses de l'université Paris-Sorbonne, 2017.

Bat, Jean-Pierre, and Pascal Geneste. "Jean Mauricheau-Beaupré: De Fontaine à Mathurin, JMB au service du Général." *Relations internationales*, no. 142 (2010): 87–100.
Baulin, Jacques. *La politique africaine d'Houphouët-Boigny.* Eurafor-Press, 1980.
Baulin, Jacques. *La politique intérieure d'Houphouët-Boigny.* Eurafor-Press, 1982.
Baulin, Jacques. *La succession d'Houphouët-Boigny.* Éditions Eurafor-Press, 1989.
Benoist, Joseph-Roger. *L'Afrique occidentale française: De la conférence de Brazzaville (1944) à l'indépendance (1960).* Les Nouvelles Editions Africaines, 1982.
Brunschwig, Henri. "The Decolonization of French Black Africa." In Gifford and Louis, *Transfer of Power in Africa.*
Bruyère-Ostells, Walter. "Outil militaire et politique africaine de la France depuis 1960: Tableau historiographique et perspectives de recherche." *Relations internationales,* no. 165 (2016): 3–22.
Chafer, Tony. *The End of Empire in French West Africa: France's Successful Decolonization?* Berg, 2002.
Chafer, Tony. "*Françafrique.*" In *Routledge Handbook of Francophone Africa,* edited by Tony Chafer and Margaret A. Majumdar. Routledge, 2023.
Chafer, Tony, and Alexander Keese, eds. *Francophone Africa at Fifty.* Manchester University Press, 2013.
Charbonneau, Bruno. *France and the New Imperialism: Security Policy in Sub-Saharan Africa.* Ashgate, 2008.
Chipman, John. *French Power in Africa.* Basil Blackwell, 1989.
Clapham, Christopher. *Africa and the International System: The Politics of State Survival.* Cambridge University Press, 1996.

Cooper, Frederick. *Africa in the World: Capitalism, Empire, Nation-State.* Harvard University Press, 2014.

Cooper, Frederick. *Africa Since 1940: The Past of the Present.* Cambridge University Press, 2002.

Cooper, Frederick. *Decolonization and African Society: The Labor Question in French and British Africa.* Cambridge University Press, 1996.

Coquery-Vidrovitch, Catherine. "La politique africaine de la France au sud du Sahara: De la conférence de Brazzaville à la Communauté." In Oulmont and Vaïsse, *De Gaulle et la décolonisation.*

Crocker, Chester A. "Military Dependence: The Colonial Legacy in Africa." *Journal of Modern African Studies* 12, no. 2 (1974): 265–86.

David, Philippe. *La Côte d'Ivoire.* Karthala, 2009.

Deltombe, Thomas. *L'Afrique d'abord! Quand François Mitterrand voulait sauver l'Empire français.* La Découverte, 2024.

Desgrandchamps, Marie-Luce. *L'humanitaire en guerre civile: La crise du Biafra (1967–1970).* Presses universitaires de Rennes, 2018.

Desgrandchamps, Marie-Luce. "Soutien militaire et aide humanitaire: Les ambiguïtés de la France au Biafra." *Relations internationales,* no. 165 (2016): 81–96.

Diallo, Siradiou. *Houphouët-Boigny, le médecin, le planteur et le ministre: 1900–1960.* Groupe jeune Afrique, 1993.

Diarra, Samba. *Les faux complots d'Houphouët-Boigny: Fracture dans le destin d'une nation (1959–1970).* Editions Karthala, 1997.

Domergue-Cloarec, Danielle. *La France et l'Afrique après les indépendances.* Sedes, 1994.

Dumbuya, Peter A. "The United States and West Africa: The Institutionalization of Foreign Relations in an

Age of Ideological Ferment." In *The United States and West Africa: Interactions and Relations*, edited by Alusine Jalloh and Toyin Falola. University of Rochester Press, 2008.

Durand, Pierre-Michel. *L'Afrique et les relations franco-américaines des années soixante: Aux origines de l'obsession américaine.* L'Harmattan, 2007.

Durand, Pierre-Michel. "De Gaulle et les Américains en Afrique subsaharienne." In Oulmont and Vaïsse, *De Gaulle et la décolonisation.*

Echenberg, Myron. "'Promotion africaine': The Africanization of Military Officers and Decolonization in French West Africa 1945–1960." In Ageron and Michel, *L'Afrique noire française.*

Evrard, Camille. "Retour sur la construction des relations militaires franco-africaines." *Relations internationales,* no. 165 (2016): 23–42.

Fauré, Y.-A., and Jean-François Médard, eds. *Etat et bourgeoisie en Côte d'Ivoire.* Karthala, 1982.

Gadji Dagbo, Joseph. *L'Affaire Kragbé Gnagbé, 32 ans après.* NEI, 2002.

Gary-Tounkara, Daouda. "Cinquante ans de politiques de la nationalité en Côte d'Ivoire." *Outre-Mers* 98, nos. 368–369 (2010): 159–75.

Gbagbo, Laurent. *Côte d'Ivoire: Pour une alternative démocratique.* L'Harmattan, 1983.

Gbagbo, Laurent. *La Côte d'Ivoire: Économie et société à la veille de l'indépendance (1940–1960).* L'Harmattan, 1982.

Geneste, Pascal. "Jacques Foccart ou la politique africaine de la France gaullienne." In Oulmont and Vaïsse, *De Gaulle et la décolonisation.*

Gifford, Prosser, and William Roger Louis, eds. *The Transfer of Power in Africa: Decolonization 1940–1960.* Yale University Press, 1982.

Ginio, Ruth. "Marshal Petain Spoke to Schoolchildren: Vichy Propaganda in French West Africa, 1940–1943." *International Journal of African Historical Studies* 33, no. 2 (2000): 291–312.
Glaser, Antoine. *AfricaFrance: Quand les dirigeants africains deviennent les maîtres du jeu.* Librairie Arthème Fayard / Pluriel, 2017.
Gould, Michael. *The Biafran War: The Struggle for Modern Nigeria.* I. B. Tauris, 2013.
Grah Mel, Frédéric. *Félix Houphouët-Boigny.* 3 vols. Editions du CERAP and Maisonneuve et Larose, 2003–10.
Grah Mel, Frédéric. "Félix Houphouët-Boigny, le ministre français qui est devenu chef d'Etat en Côte d'Ivoire." In Bat et al., *Jacques Foccart.*
Granvaud, Raphaël, and David Mauger. *Un pompier pyromane: L'ingérence française en Côte d'Ivoire d'Houphouët-Boigny à Ouattara.* Agone, 2018.
Gregory, Shaun. "The French Military in Africa: Past and Present." *African Affairs* 99, no. 396 (2000): 435–48.
Griffin, Christopher. "French Military Policy in the Nigerian Civil War, 1967–1970." *Small Wars and Insurgencies* 26, no. 1 (2015): 114–35.
Grilli, Matteo. *Nkrumaism and African Nationalism: Ghana's Pan-African Foreign Policy in the Age of Decolonization.* Palgrave Macmillan, 2018.
Guilhaume, Philippe. "Les relations entre la France et la Côte d'Ivoire (1960–1978)." PhD diss., Institut d'études politiques de Paris, 1979.
Guisnel, Jean. "Derrière la guerre du Biafra, la France." In *Histoire secrète de la Ve République,* edited by Roger Faligot and Jean Guisnel. La Découverte, 2006.

Hanretta, Sean. "'To Never Shed Blood': Yacouba Sylla, Félix Houphouët-Boigny and Islamic Modernization in Côte d'Ivoire." *Journal of African History* 49, no. 2 (2008): 281–304.

Harshé, Rajen. *Pervasive Entente: France and Ivory Coast in African Affairs.* Gulab Varzirani, 1984.

Heimann, Gadi. "A Case of Diplomatic Symbiosis: France, Israel and the Former French Colonies, 1958–1962." *Journal of Contemporary History* 51, no. 1 (2016): 145–64.

Hofnung, Thomas. *La crise ivoirienne: De Félix Houphouët-Boigny à la chute de Laurent Gbagbo.* La Découverte, 2011.

Keese, Alexander. *Living with Ambiguity: Integrating an African Elite in French and Portuguese Africa, 1930–61.* Franz Steiner Verlag, 2007.

Kent, John. *The Internationalization of Colonialism: Britain, France, and Black Africa, 1939–1956.* Clarendon, 1992.

Kipre, Pierre, and Alain Tirefort. "La Côte d'Ivoire." In *L'Afrique occidentale au temps des français: Colonisateurs et colonisés (c. 1860–1960),* edited by Coquery-Vidrovitch. Éditions La Découverte, 1992.

Koffi Koffi, Lazare. *La France contre la Côte d'Ivoire: L'affaire du Sanwi; Du malentendu politico-juridique à la tentative de sécession.* L'Harmattan, 2013.

Koné, Amadou. *Houphouët-Boigny et la crise ivoirienne.* Karthala, 2003.

Konieczna, Anna. "L'Afrique du Sud, un partenaire particulier pour le 'dialogue.'" In Bat et al., *Jacques Foccart.*

Konieczna, Anna. "L'Histoire d'une 'relation spéciale': Les relations entre la France et l'Afrique du Sud dans les années 1958–1974." PhD diss., Sciences Po Paris, 2013.

Labrune-Badiane, Céline, and Etienne Smith. *Les Hussards noirs de la colonie: Instituteurs africains et "petites patries" en AOF (1913–1960).* Karthala, 2018.

Lawler, Nancy Ellen. *Soldiers of Misfortune: Ivoirien Tirailleurs of World War II.* Ohio University Press, 1992.

Legvold, Robert. *Soviet Policy in West Africa.* Harvard University Press, 1970.

Léopold Sédar Senghor: La pensée et l'action politique; Actes du colloque organisé par la section française de l'Assemblée parlementaire de la Francophonie. Assemblée Nationale and Organisation Internationale de la Francophonie, 2006.

Lopez, Robert. *Au temps banni d'Houphouët-Boigny: Côte d'Ivoire, France, regards croisés.* L'Harmattan, 2006.

Luckham, Robin. "French Militarism in Africa." *Review of African Political Economy* 9, no. 24 (1982): 55–84.

Manning, Patrick. *Francophone Sub-Saharan Africa 1880–1995.* Cambridge University Press, 1998.

Martin, Garret Joseph. *General de Gaulle's Cold War: Challenging American Hegemony, 1963–1968.* Berghahn, 2013.

Mazov, Sergey. *A Distant Front in the Cold War: The USSR in West Africa and the Congo, 1956–1964.* Woodrow Wilson Center Press and Stanford University Press, 2010.

Meignan, Gouédan Richard. "La réinstauration du multipartisme: L'ultime sacrifice du président Félix Houphouët-Boigny pour la paix en Côte d'Ivoire." *Revue ivoirienne d'histoire,* no. 31 (2018): 114–25.

Mélandri, Pierre. "Les Etats-Unis et les indépendances africaines." In Ageron and Michel, *L'Afrique noire française.*

Meriwether, James H. "'A Torrent Overrunning Everything': Africa and the Eisenhower Administration." In *The Eisenhower Administration, the Third World, and the Globalization of the Cold War,* edited by Kathryn C. Statler and Andrew L. Johns. Rowman & Littlefield, 2006.

Michel, Marc. "De Gaulle, l'Afrique et les Africains depuis Brazzaville." In Oulmont and Vaïsse, *De Gaulle et la décolonisation.*

Michel, Marc. "L'Afrique noire, la France et la Grande-Bretagne en 1958: L'accélération des indépendances et la sauvegarde des 'French and English Connections.'" In Ageron and Michel, *L'Afrique noire française.*

Migani, Guia. *La France et l'Afrique sub-saharienne, 1957–1963: Histoire d'une décolonisation entre idéaux eurafricains et politique de puissance.* Peter Lang, 2008.

Morris-Jones, W. H., Georges Fischer, eds. *Decolonisation and After: The British and French Experience.* Frank Cass, 1980.

Mousset, Paul. "La République de M. Houphouët-Boigny à l'heure de l'indépendance." *Revue des Deux Mondes,* 15 September 1960, 254–70.

Muehlenbeck, Philip E. *Betting on the Africans: John F. Kennedy's Courting of African Nationalist Leaders.* Oxford University Press, 2012.

Muehlenbeck, Philip E. *Czechoslovakia in Africa, 1945–1968.* Palgrave Macmillan, 2016.

Namikas, Lise. *Battleground Africa: Cold War in the Congo, 1960–1965.* Woodrow Wilson Center Press and Stanford University Press, 2013.

Nandjui, Pierre. *Houphouët-Boigny: L'homme de la France en Afrique.* L'Harmattan, 1995.

Nwaubani, Ebere. *The United States and Decolonization in West Africa.* University of Rochester Press, 2001.
Osseo-Asare, Abena Dove. *Atomic Junction: Nuclear Power in Africa After Independence.* Cambridge University Press, 2019.
Oulmont, Philippe, and Maurice Vaïsse, eds. *De Gaulle et la décolonisation de l'Afrique subsaharienne.* Karthala, 2014.
Pascallon, Pierre, ed. *La politique de sécurité de la France en Afrique.* L'Harmattan, 2004.
Péan, Pierre. *L'homme de l'ombre: Eléments d'enquête autour de Jacques Foccart, l'homme le plus mystérieux et le plus puissant de la Ve République.* Fayard, 1990.
Porter Sanchez, Danielle. "The Brazzaville Conference and the Future of French Colonialism in Africa." In *The Routledge Handbook of French History.* Routledge, 2024.
Prosperetti, Elisa. "The Hidden History of the West African Wager: Or, How Comparison with Ghana Made Côte d'Ivoire." *History in Africa* 45 (2018): 29–57.
Rabinowitz, Beth S. *Coups, Rivals, and the Modern State: Why Rural Coalitions Matter in Sub-Saharan Africa.* Cambridge University Press, 2018.
Reynolds, Jonathan T. *Sovereignty and Struggle: Africa and Africans in the Era of the Cold War, 1945–1994.* Oxford University Press, 2015.
Roche, Christian. *50 ans d'indépendance dans les anciennes possessions françaises d'Afrique noire.* L'Harmattan, 2011.
Schmidt, Elizabeth. *Cold War and Decolonization in Guinea, 1946–1958.* Ohio University Press, 2007.
Schmidt, Elizabeth. *Foreign Intervention in Africa: From the Cold War to the War on Terror.* Cambridge University Press, 2013.

Schraeder, Peter J. "Cold War to Cold Peace: Explaining U.S.-French Competition in Francophone Africa." *Political Science Quarterly* 115, no. 3 (2000): 395–419.

Semley, Lorelle. *To Be Free and French: Citizenship in France's Atlantic Empire.* Cambridge University Press, 2017.

Simonet, Thibaut. "Les composantes du pouvoir de Félix Houphouët-Boigny en Côte d'Ivoire (1958–1965)." *Outre-Mers* 98, no. 368–369 (2010): 403–20.

Siriex, Paul-Henri. *Félix Houphouët-Boigny: L'homme de la paix.* Nouvelles Éditions Africaines, 1975.

Siriex, Paul-Henri. *Houphouët-Boigny ou la sagesse africaine.* Éditions Nathan and Nouvelles Éditions Africaines, 1986.

Smith, Tony. "Patterns in the Transfer of Power: A Comparative Study of French and British Decolonization." In Gifford and Louis, *Transfer of Power in Africa.*

St. Jorre, John de. *The Brothers' War: Biafra and Nigeria.* 1972. Repr., Faber and Faber, 2009.

Statler, Kathryn C., and Andrew L. Johns, eds. *The Eisenhower Administration, the Third World, and the Globalization of the Cold War.* Rowman & Littlefield, 2006.

Stremlau, John J. *The International Politics of the Nigerian Civil War, 1967–1970.* Princeton University Press, 1977.

Teya, Koffi Pascal. *Côte d'Ivoire: Le roi est nu.* L'Harmattan, 1985.

Thomas, Martin. *Fight or Flight: Britain, France, and Their Roads from Empire.* Oxford University Press, 2014.

Thomas, Martin. "Innocent Abroad? Decolonisation and US Engagement with French West Africa,

1945–56." *Journal of Imperial and Commonwealth History* 36, no. 1 (2008): 47–73.

Thomas, Martin, Bob Moore, L. J. Butler. *Crises of Empire: Decolonization and Europe's Imperial States, 1918–1975*. Hodder Education, 2008.

Thompson, Virginia. *West Africa's Council of the Entente*. Cornell University Press, 1972.

Toungara, Jeanne Maddox. "The Apotheosis of Côte d'Ivoire's Nana Houphouët-Boigny." *Journal of Modern African Studies* 28, no. 1 (1990): 23–54.

Treacher, Adrian. *French Interventionism: Europe's Last Global Player?* Ashgate, 2003.

Turpin, Frédéric. "1958, la Communauté franco-africaine: Un projet de puissance entre héritages de la IVe République et conceptions gaulliennes." *Outre-Mers* 96, no. 358–359 (2008): 45–58.

Turpin, Frédéric. *De Gaulle, Pompidou et l'Afrique: Décoloniser et coopérer (1958–1974)*. Les Indes savantes, 2010.

Turpin, Frédéric. *Jacques Foccart: Dans l'ombre du pouvoir.* CNRS Éditions, 2015.

Turtio, Riina. *State-Building and National Militaries in Postcolonial West Africa: Decolonizing the Means of Coercion 1958–1974*. James Currey, 2023.

Vaïsse, Maurice. *La grandeur: Politique étrangère du général de Gaulle 1958–1969*. Fayard, 1998.

Vaïsse, Maurice. *La puissance ou l'influence? La France dans le monde depuis 1958*. Fayard, 2009.

Warson, Joanna. "Beyond Co-Operation and Competition: Anglo-French Relations, Connected Histories of Decolonization and Rhodesia's Unilateral Declaration of Independence, 1965–80." *Historical Research* 88, no. 242 (2015): 740–64.

Warson, Joanna. "France in Rhodesia: French Policy and Perceptions Throughout the Era of

Decolonisation." PhD diss., University of Portsmouth, 2013.
Wauthier, Claude. "Jacques Foccart et les mauvais conseils de Félix Houphouët-Boigny." *Les Cahiers du centre de recherches historiques,* no. 30 (2002). https://doi.org/10.4000/ccrh.512.
Wilder, Gary. *Freedom Time: Negritude, Decolonization, and the Future of the World.* Duke University Press, 2015.
Woronoff, Jon. *West African Wager: Houphouët Versus Nkrumah.* Scarecrow Press, 1972.
Wyss, Marco. "The Gendarme Stays in Africa: France's Military Role in Côte d'Ivoire." *African Conflict and Peacebuilding Review* 3, no. 1 (2013): 81–111.
Wyss, Marco. "Neo-Imperial Cold War? Biafra's Franco-African Arms Triangle." *Journal of African History* 65, no. 1 (2024): 47–65.
Wyss, Marco. "The Nkrumah Factor: The Strategic Alignment of Early Postcolonial Côte d'Ivoire and Nigeria." *English Historical Review* 138, no. 592 (2023): 591–619.
Wyss, Marco. *Postcolonial Security: Britain, France, and West Africa's Cold War.* Oxford University Press, 2021.
Wyss, Marco. "*Primus inter Pares?* France and Multi-Actor Peacekeeping in Côte d'Ivoire." In *Peacekeeping in Africa: The Evolving Security Architecture,* edited by Thierry Tardy and Marco Wyss. Routledge, 2014.
Ziké, Marc A. *La politique étrangère de la Côte d'Ivoire (1959–1993): Une diplomatie au service de la paix et du développement.* COPRECA Edition, 1994.
Zolberg, Aristide R. *One-Party Government in the Ivory Coast.* 2nd ed. Princeton University Press, 1969.
Zolberg, Aristide R., and Philip Foster. *Ghana and the Ivory Coast: Perspectives on Modernization.* University of Chicago Press, 1971.

Index

Printed and bound by CPI Group (UK) Ltd, Croydon, CR0 4YY

21/09/2026

14965993-0001